A Tool for Learning

A TOOL FOR LEARNING

MAURICE RUBENS   MARY NEWLAND
M.B.E.

There is a form of pedagogical romanticism that urges an arousal of unconscious, creative impulses in the child as an aid to learning. One would do well to be cautious about such doctrine. Unconscious impulses unconstrained by awareness can be quite the contrary of creative.
Jerome S, Bruner, Towards a Theory of Instruction, 1971.

Published with assistance from The Calouste Gulbenkian Foundation

A Tool for Learning was designed and edited by Maurice Rubens and published with assistance from The Calouste Gulbenkian Foundation by the authors Maurice Rubens and Mary Newland through Direct Experience, 18 Anglesea Road, Ipswich IP1 3PP.

ISBN 0 9514026 0 9 A Tool for Learning (pbk).

Printed in Great Britian by
Richard Clay Ltd, Bungay, Suffolk

British Library Cataloguing in Publication Data

Rubens, Maurice,
   A tool for learning: some functions of art
in primary education
   1. Primary schools. Curriculum subjects:
Art. Teaching
   I. Title   II. Newland, Mary, *M.B.E.*
   372.2'044

ISBN 0-9514026-0-9

Copyright The Authors, 1989.

FOR
JOHN F. FRIEND
1902–1988
FOUNDING PRINCIPAL BRETTON HALL COLLEGE OF EDUCATION

"What constitutes the dignity of Teaching? It is to realise that knowledge leads to understanding, and understanding is something that must be patiently and devotedly unmasked. Surely the dignity of teaching is to unmask it with simplicity, to guide the pupil into the inner centre of learning and to know that you can leave him there to browse with insight, self-assurance and discrimination" Dame Ninette de Valois, Bretton Hall 1962.

FOREWORD

In 1982, The Gulbenkian Report, The Arts in Schools stated:
"The Arts are important ways of knowing the world and of interpreting our experience in it."

It is therefore particularly fitting that the generosity of The Calouste Gulbenkian Foundation makes the timely publication of this book possible.

All engaged in education, whether teachers, parents or students will find in it helpful guidance in their search for greater visual understanding.

Mary Newland and Maurice Rubens, have through their school and centre based in-service teaching, encouraged many teachers to develop their skills and to provide the stimulating environment that allows real learning to take place. Their enthusiasm and deep personal committment to education have kindled and kept alight the same spark in others.

Here, they outline the role of Art as a means of enriching the curriculum across subject boundaries whilst emphasising its centrality within the area of aesthetic, creative learning and experience.

Too often, the functions of Art in the overall learning process are overlooked. Here, the authors attempt to show, in practical ways, how this very special tool can be used to the greatest advantage. They remind us that unless children can be offered appropriate tools and be taught the effective mastery of them, they end up with the old cry, too familiar to many adults, "I can't draw!"

Janet Bonner O.B.E.
Artist, H.M.I. (Retired)

CONTENTS

Some Functions of Art	6
Some Skills	7
Across the Curriculum	8
Stages not Ages	11
Early Expectations	12
Frog Spawn and Pond Weed	13
Learning to Look	15
Developing Writing	16
Drawing as a Tool for Learning	18
Some First-hand Experience	22
Setting the Scene	23
The Teacher's Role	24
Talk	26
Table Talk	27
Making Connections	30
Focus	31
Drawing an Object	32
Teachers as Learners	34
Seeing and Thinking	36
The Jungle	40
Making Meaning	42
Some Intentions	43
Looking at Art	44
Context and Function	46
Beyond the Classroom	47
Learning on Location	48
Before we go	51
Focusing Selecting Questioning	53
Finding our Way	54
Looking and Seeing	57
Do We Have to Draw?	58
A Historical Perspective	59
Tools	62
Paint in the Classroom	64
Expression	68
Responding to a New Experience	69
Imagination and Fantasy	70
Evaluating Art in the Primary School	74
Extending Learning Through Art	76
Some Signs of Progression	78
Looking Forward	80
A Summing Up	83
Tools for Learning	84
Afterword	88

A TOOL FOR LEARNING

An Introduction

This book proposes approaches to visual education which emphasise a personal response to direct experience and the present needs of all learners. It aims to help teachers to relate visual education to these needs and reflects an awareness of the circumstances and influences which affect our lives.

Drawing in its wider sense is proposed as a practical starting point and a tool for learning, but emphasis is also placed upon the need for some understanding of the wide range and functions of Art in all the learning areas of the Primary Curriculum.

We believe that this approach radically challenges a whole range of established ideas and attitudes to Art in education.

These traditions, for such they have become, have declined into inadequate responses to learners needs. They often produce only time-passing formulas, concerned with little more than stereotyped ornamentation, exempt from evaluation as learning.

This book aims to increase the teacher's confidence in and understanding of Art, not only as a way of learning but the equally important function of Art as an expressive discipline with its own traditions, language and values, capable of enriching all environments, societies, cultures and individuals.

The function of this book for readers, dependent on their perceptions, may be as a discussion document, an occasional reference, a framework for future activities or a foundation for guidelines.

Maurice Rubens   Mary Newland M.B.E.

SOME FUNCTIONS OF ART IN PRIMARY EDUCATION

Communicating — { Symbols, signs and marks conveying information, writing, maps, diagrams.

Investigating, Exploring, Discovering, Analysing — { Environmental, cultural, social scientific, historic perspectives.

Expressing — { Personal response to direct experience; Development from feeling to meaning.

Decorating — { Ornamenting, enhancing or enriching, with with understanding of function.

Illustrating, Recording, Recognising — { Clear visual presentation of learning; Understanding and reasoned discernment. Potential for initiation of further development in other areas of learning.

"Let us say I paint a tree, conscientiously, from my perspective view; that would be one aspect of truth, or I might paint it from several views, combining them, that might be another. A botanist and a physicist may challenge me; The botanist, 'You must give some indication of how a tree functions, how sap is carried to the leaves, how chlorophyll is manufactured, some sense of growth!' The physicist, 'You've given us nothing of its complex atomic structure. Can you ignore photo-synthesis?' They are followed by a carpenter, a priest, a poet, an ecologist..."
Ben Shahn.

"The more I draw, the more I see." Overheard in class.

"There is no kind of experience which has not its potential visual dimension or its latent meanings for literary or other expression."
Ben Shahn, (1898–1969).

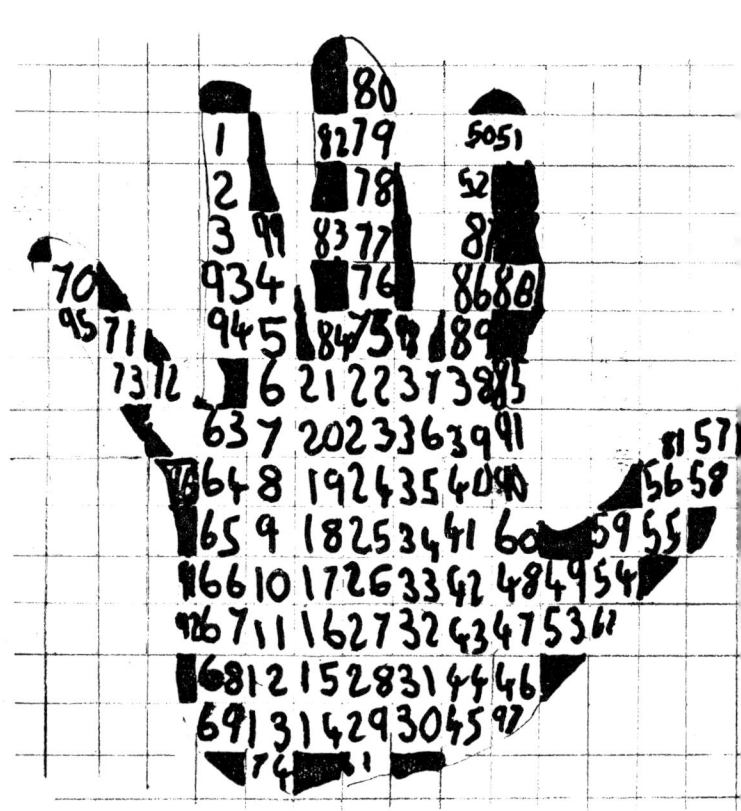

Simple graphic measurement.

Pencils

This afternoon my class did Art work. We used thick pencils. First we had paper. We used our pencil on the tip and on the side. After we drew our shoe by takeing off our shoe and studyed it. When I write I use it on the tip. When I draw I use it on the tip and on the side. We learnt of what H means. H means hard. B means black. Diffrent pressure means diffrent shades.

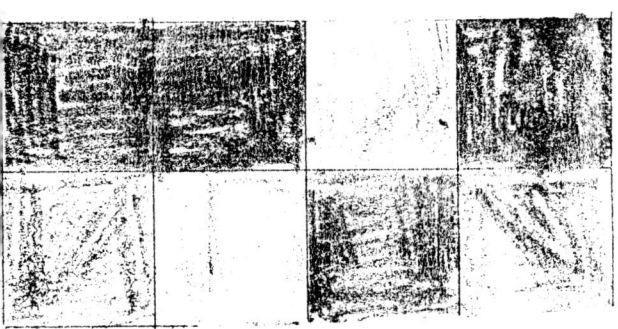

Researching tools; the pencil.

SOME SKILLS

Study skills
   Enquiry, analysis, Acquisition of knowledge. The use of resources and reference material.

Perceptual skills
   Observation and representation, discernment of differences and similarities of shape and colour; recognition and representation of order, proportion and scale.

Motor skills
   Effective use of basic tools and appropriate materials.

Design related skills
   The generation and realisation of ideas within the constraints of a material, a process or a need. Selection, adaptation.

Critical skills
   Evaluation of facts, formation of viewpoints and understanding of criteria by which teachers and learners assess learning.

Communication skills
   Development of visual and verbal competence, communicating response to experience. Understanding the particular terminology used to discuss Art and Design.

"I'm immensely fond of pencil. I like pencil to hang up in the house. I think there's something wonderful about a pencil drawing. I just draw and rub it with my finger or anything else and then fiddle with it. I think 'fiddle with it' is the right term until I get it right. Draw, then start getting tone by your finger, your pencil, india rubber of course, until it has eased up and you get it right."
L. S. Lowry. 1887–1976.

Mr Ayling

Mr Ayling is the schoolkeeper. The most important thing he does is delivering the milks into all the classes in the school. This term Mr Ayling mended our blackboard. He brings cupboards into all the classrooms. Mr Ayling paints the lines in the playground. He rings the bell and cleans the toilets

A TOOL FOR LEARNING ACROSS THE CURRICULUM

As so many learning experiences are initiated, developed, assimilated and reinforced visually, Art can be used as a learning tool in almost every area of the Primary School Curriculum.

Much of the work shown in these pages is the outcome of learners' experience outside the framework of an "Art lesson". Examples may be found that demonstrate the beginnings of real learning in Maths, Science, History and above all, a growing competence in the use of language.

Cross-curricular references should, if possible avoid token *Arts Integration*. Integration stems from the Latin "integrare", meaning "to make whole". Dance, Drama, Music and Art are not incomplete modes of representing experience. The task of the teacher is to clarify and deepen understanding, not to promote superficiality.

The visual events on the opposite page were all encountered within five minutes walk from inner city schools. They might serve as starting points for learning in many curriculum areas and at different stages of development. This will depend upon the learners' previous experience, present skills and available resources.

A prime need is appropriate reference material.

"Seeing comes before words. The child looks and recognises before it can speak. But there is another sense in which seeing comes before words. It is seeing which establishes our place in the surrounding world."
John Berger, Ways of Seeing, 1972.

STAGES NOT AGES

This composite chart illustrates a few of the most commonly encountered markmaking stages in childrens rapid progress through early developmental stages. Children are born learners.

Growing control of a tool is clearly seen, as is the increasing awareness of the environment.

The first marks are important traces of learning through direct experience. We are accustomed to call it scribble. Young children seem to have an unselfconscious confidence in their ability to respond to stimulus and learn.

When the marks begin to stand for, or signify meaning, the child is still not primarily concerned with communicating or making images. As proud parents or teachers we are eager to grab the results and pin them on the wall, though the child often discards or superimposes drawings.

The functions and meanings of this activity change when the child encounters the socialising experience of school. Here images command values, are negotiable and can be shared.

The later stage reached and represented by "A" is typical. This child has attained a virtual peak in terms of motor skills.

Almost all the dexterity and precision ever likely to be required have been acquired.

This stage often coincides with the learner's dissatisfaction. "I can't get it right," is heard.

Many learners fail to develop beyond this stage. The next drawing is by a lady of 75 (B).

Some learners remain deprived of a major tool for learning. The sensitive teacher will at least be aware of some of the causes of this stumbling block.

The learner needs, at this stage, to be helped towards an awareness that there are always a number of "right" solutions to each problem.

Before children have made their first mark, from the moment their eyes open, they are bombarded with images. These images, in countless, bewildering and varied visual languages, carry powerfully conditioning messages. The 40ft. long king-size cigarette, the garishly over-dressed bunny, Rambo and the singing dancing flowerpot have various functions, but have only one thing in common.

They come from grown-ups and are "right". We live in a "Daddy knows best" society. Indeed, in our culture, some images are more "right" than others. We are told the camera cannot lie. (It is in fact, all it can do.)

When children reach the stage when particular experiences call for individual responses, they may no longer have the confidence to trust the evidence of their own direct experience.

We all need to develop and encourage a critical, discerning and questioning attitude to visual experience. To become visually literate.

Here, the last drawings, show children responding to life with some of the confidence we see in the earliest scribble. The teacher's task is, as always, to assist the learner's autonomous development.

EARLY EXPECTATIONS

Young children respond to experience. Their responses relate to concepts like size and shape, hardness and softness.

Their first markmaking represents the traces that their ordering leaves as evidence.

Gradually, as skills develop, young children move from this self-centredness and respond to the viewpoints of others. They begin to see connections and make comparisons. The teacher must be aware of the child's developing range of skills, including an increasing ability to observe. The child also becomes more confident in the use of markmaking as expressive communication.

Children do not develop according to exact categories and the teacher learns to teach by closely watching and listening. Younger children are happier with tools that make strong, immediate statements (like fibre-tip pens).

Older children still enjoy using these but are soon ready to test a wider range of graphic media (a range of graded pencils 2B–6B, Biros, chalk, charcoal, crayon, pen and ink).

For the teacher not discouraged by low expectations, nor over anxious to produce end-products, the lack of "Art Training" is not a handicap.

The first drawing is by a 5 year old. This stage was described by Rhoda Kellogg as "typical drawing made of scribbles". It shows considerable control and order.

The second drawing by a child at the same stage shows the skills extended and the attention span considerably prolonged. This drawing was made while examining and discussing sunflower heads from the school garden.

"The process of drawing, painting or constructing is a complex one in which the child brings together diverse elements of his experience to make a new and meaningful whole. In the process of selecting, interpreting and reforming these elements, he has given us more than a picture or a sculpture; he has given us a part of himself; how he thinks, how he feels and how he sees."
"The term 'self-expression' has often been misunderstood. Self-expression is giving vent in constructive forms to the feelings, emotions and thoughts of an individual at his own level of development. What matters is the mode of expression, not the content. It is important to mention this, because one of the greatest mistakes that can be made in the use of the term 'self-expression' is to think of it in terms of an unstructured or uncontrolled emotion, or, on the other hand, to consider it as mere imitation."
Victor Lowenfeld and W. Lambert Brittain. Creative and Mental Growth, 1969.

 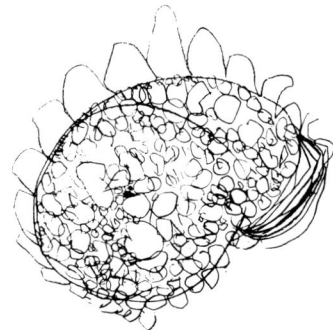

FROG-SPAWN AND POND WEED

This illustration was not taken from a school.

It was found in a front garden.

Without much guesswork, it might be traced to a presumably educational source. There are clues. Examined as evidence, it would seem at least two people were involved. A young child, for the painting and an adult, for the writing and of course for the provision of paper, brush and paint. On further enquiry we might well be told that Kerry was learning through Art.

Learning about using tools, learning about colour, learning to express herself. This may be so. If it is, then this record of learning is far too valuable to be left to blow about in the garden. Let the enquiry be directed towards more precise questions.

What is Kerry doing? What does she think she is doing? Has she done it before? Will she do it again? How long was she engaged? What choices or decisions was she able to make? What experience did she have? What did she understand? Had she completed the activity? What will she do next? Finally, what was and what will be expected?

As Kerry continues through school she will spend considerable time on similar activities especially at Christmas and Halloween. Towards the end of her Junior School years she will do less. She will be less willing to spare the time when more engaging and rewarding activities are filling the timetable.

In her first three secondary years, the position is likely to be formalised. She will spend forty-five minutes each week on Art activities. If she is disturbed or disruptive, the time may be doubled, for the subject is believed to be soothing and undemanding.

At the end of the third year of Secondary School, Kerry and two-thirds of her classmates will abandon the subject for ever.

The surviving third, continuing for two more years, will now be subject to a new element, critical evaluation. The evaluative criteria are usually brought in from outside the school. Up to this point the subject has been virtually evaluation free. Exempt that is from any questioning more precise than: Is it nice? Do you like it? Do I like it? Does it express what you feel? Such criteria, applied across the curriculum would produce a curious image of learning.

The outside examining body will bring to bear a range of Art based criteria which, appropriate or not, have rarely, if ever been previously applied.

A small proportion of the survivors continue to pursue the subject on these terms for a further two years. Some rare spirits persist even longer, a few until they cease to be learners and die.

The indications are that this is a systematic, cumulative and wasteful rejection of a subject area that has served its purpose. Or failed to serve its purpose. Or its purpose has been misunderstood. The subject is Art. Many pupils, teachers and parents are confused as to its functions in education.

If we believe that Art is and always has been a most powerful tool for learning, then the centrality of its place in the curriculum must be considered.

The second illustration is from a learning stage comparable to that of Kerry. This time the learner has written her name as part of the activity. She has used a precise and controlled tool. The white paper allows the marks she has made to be clearly seen. She has particular concerns, intentions and interests. She has been engaged for a considerable time. Through looking, she is likely to have understood something of the experience which her drawing records.

We should be concerned that, for all we know, Kerry was attempting, with slight possibility of success, to respond to an experience at least as complex as frog spawn and pond weed.

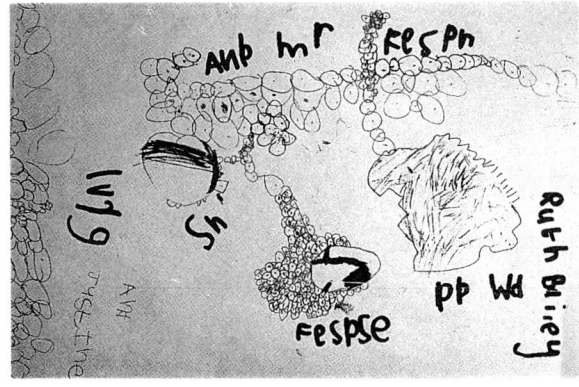

"In learning to draw you learn to look. You teach yourself to see and to feel what you see. Drawing is a more interesting way than writing of passing on feelings about the world you see because it is closer to what we actually feel."
David Hockney in Jeffery Camp's book "Draw", 1984.

LEARNING TO LOOK

Looking leads to the ability to express responses, visually, verbally, technically, literally, factually and personally. Looking leads to scientific, linguistic, spiritual and historical experiences.

Looking promotes comparison and discernment.

Direct experience strengthens meaning, reinforces skills and may lead towards expression.

Children who learn to look, learn to question, to discover and to understand.

Looking through drawing, prolongs the looking.

Looking encourages concentration.

Looking absorbs, engages, calms and sensitises the learner.

"It has been sagaciously discerned by Simonides or else discovered by some other person, that the most complete pictures are formed in our minds of the things that have been conveyed to them and imprinted on them by the senses, but that the keenest of all our senses is the sense of sight, and that consequently perceptions received by the ears or by reflexion can be most easily retained if they are also conveyed to our minds by the mediation of the eyes."
Cicero, De Oratore II, IXXXVII, 357.

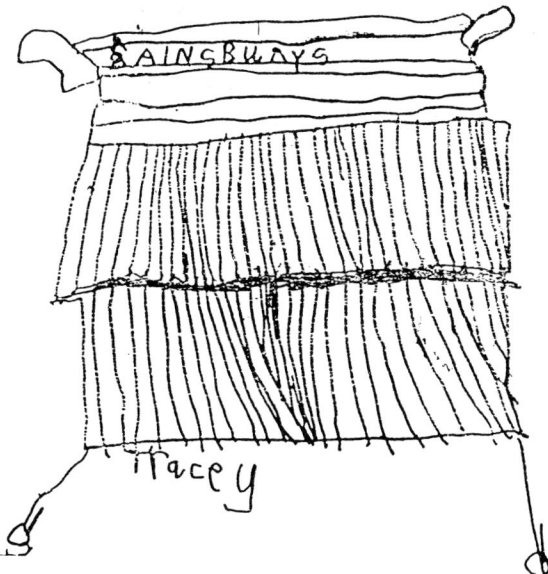

DEVELOPING WRITING – DEVELOPING DRAWING

Some Parallels

During the academic year 1983–84 four teachers from an Inner London primary school had attended courses on writing and as a result introduced a developmental approach to writing in their classrooms. They would define developmental writing as writing that progresses in direct relation to a child's conceptual development.

The resulting work generated much interest among colleagues and led to a series of staff meetings in the Spring of 1985 to discuss this particular approach. Subsequently a unanimous decision was taken to adopt a developmental approach to writing as a whole school policy.

Parallels with drawing development were noted and the cross-curricular work plans involved developing the children's graphic skills.

The work shown here is based on this approach which places emphasis on the idea of self-correction as crucial to linguistic learning, sustaining a proper faith in children's ability to teach themselves.

The notion of self-regulation, i.e. the task under the control of the learner, can be more readily fostered within a developmental framework.

The conventions of the language system are not imposed upon the learner who is hypothesising about how the written language works, initially using very limited knowledge.

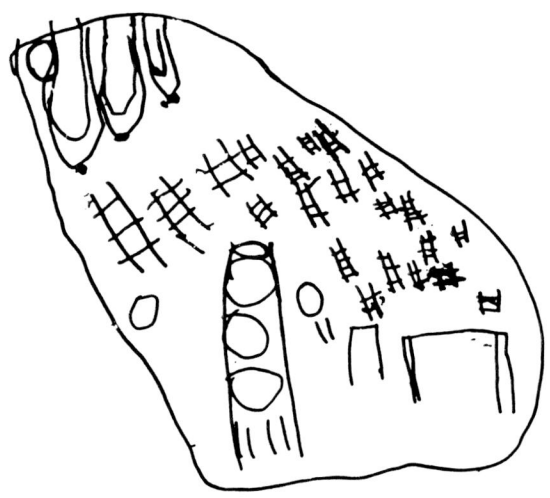

Gradually, with appropriate teacher intervention, the child moves closer towards standard written English.

Children are encouraged to use written language in any way they can as soon as they enter school, they do not have to wait until they can write correctly before writing. They are helped to understand that writing is a tool that they can use for a variety of purposes.

A cross-curricular development of writing and drawing reveals the wide range of developmental stages encountered and some links between these stages in writing and drawing can be observed.

With rapidly developing skills, children move through a self-centred stage of development and begin to respond to the attitudes and view-points of others. They begin to make comparisons and to see visual and linguistic relationships.

When the child is confident in the use of words and mark making tools, the promotion of more conscious learning becomes appropriate. The child's own work is the source of the teaching point used to promote his/her individual development and understanding of language.

A teacher, sensitive to learners' responses, becomes adept at guiding their paths of enquiry, helping them to recognise new concepts and to make decisions for themselves.

The traces of learning experience, whether written, drawn or as in the present case, both, are indispensable for the Primary School Teacher.

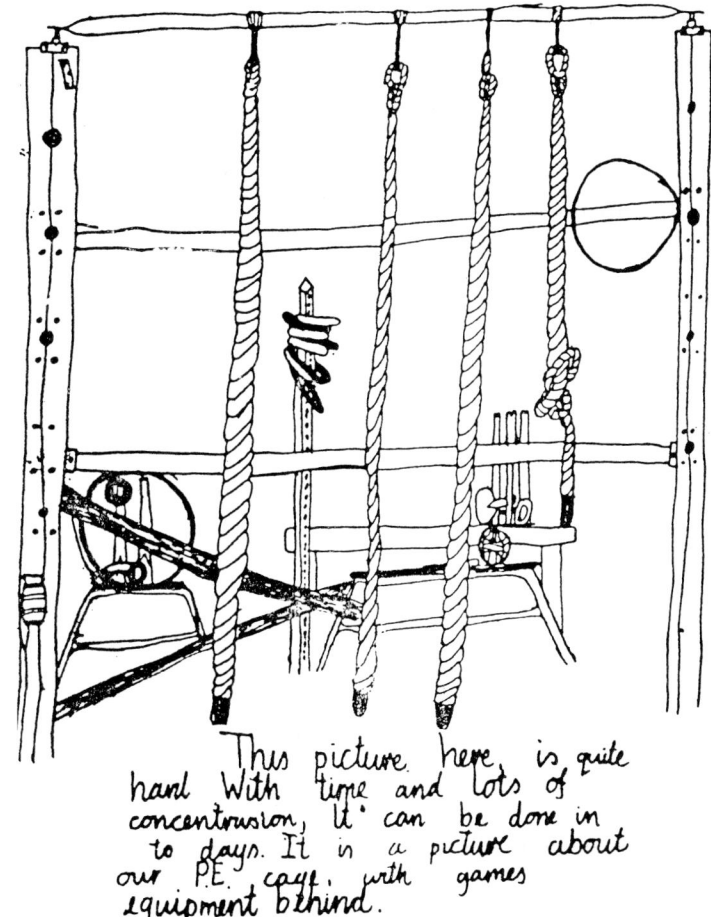

This picture here, is quite hard with time and lots of concentration, it can be done in to days. It is a picture about our P.E. cage, with games equipment behind.

DRAWING AS A TOOL FOR LEARNING

Art as a mode of thought (or learning tool), may be most clearly understood through an examination of drawing.

To draw (from the Old H. German, *tragen*), is primarily a gestural, ordering act. Think of drawing a cart, drawing water.

When we come to the expressive or externalising properties of Art and consider the traces that record the gesture, we encounter the more generally accepted meaning.

Drawing as marks, recording, representing and signifying

Many learning experiences are initiated, developed and assimilated visually

If a learner is able to confidently record developing awareness, i.e. knowledge, it follows that capacity for learning is enhanced. Developing children need the support of a perceptive teacher when they feel they are unable to represent their world as they experience it and as they see it represented in the images of others. It takes time, practice, skill and confidence to scan or read even a simple object and to learn more from it.

Drawing keeps the eye engaged and is an excellent starting point in deciphering an unfamiliar object visually.

The act of converting an idea into lines and other marks on paper often excites the mind and frees the imagination, encouraging the flow of creative thought.

The pencil's purpose is not to "teach drawing". Its purpose is to hold the learner longer in the presence, to prolong the period of attentive looking and to allow time to relate what is known, told or seen.

New ideas are promoted, leading to greater understanding.

Children can be helped to use drawing as a means of discovery

A process to assist learning

This Infant class were stimulated by their discovery of nest building materials in the school garden. This enabled them to make more sense of the stuffed birds when they came to make simple prints later in the term.

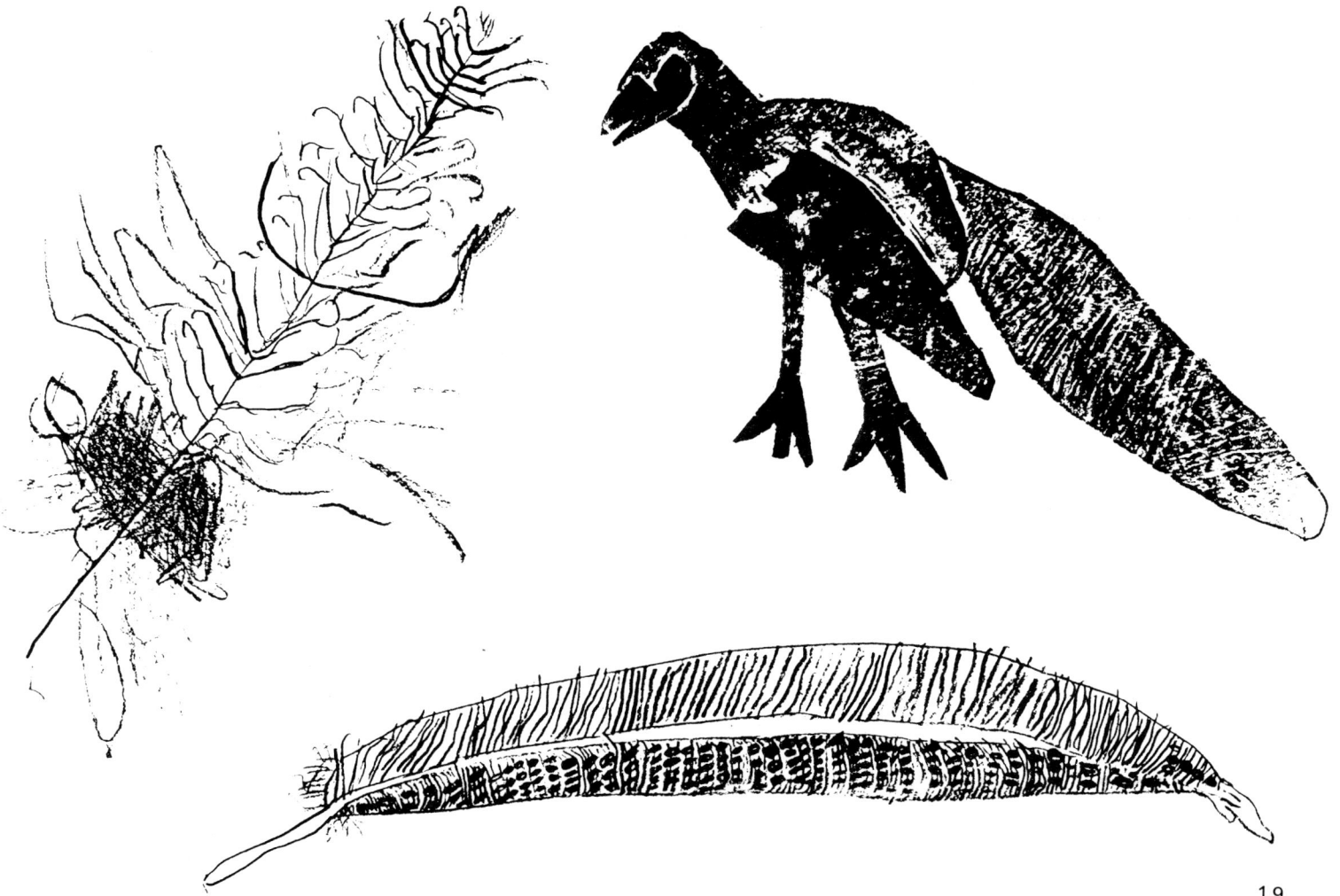

This London primary school is fortunate to have a large garden which involves the children at many points in their learning.

Here, the preliminary studies were embarked on with the intention of painting.

This led to a much closer examination of particular plants and eventually to the expression of personal responses to the common environment.

"On mallow flowers there are five petals which are heartshaped ... The light and dark purple petals are soft and silky, the stalk is rough and furry ... The petals looked like purple hearts flying in the air ... The new mallows look like the cones we play with in P.E. ... The dead ones look like poles ... The poppies were dark pink and red with some purple ... The stalk is prickly but the cup of petals is very soft and smooth ... It looks like a ballerina ... Inside are little seeds ... When you tip the dried poppy head up-side down the seeds drop out ... The roses had fragile pink petals ... Very delicate and breakable ... The leaves are hard ... When the petals have fallen off they leave rose hips ... The rose hips are hard and strong ... They are yellow, pink and red ... The thorns are shaped like horns ...

SOME FIRST-HAND EXPERIENCE

None of us have met Henry the Eighth but Hans Holbein did. He left us a record of this direct, first hand and probably uncomfortable experience. A clear reproduction of this drawing could be described as "First-rate, second hand" source material.

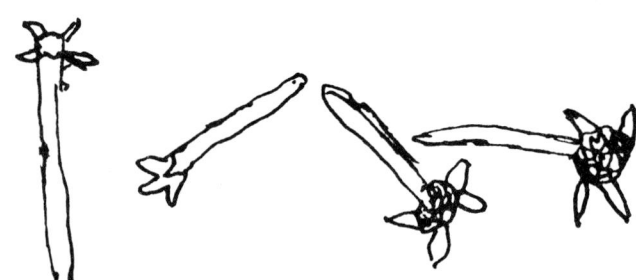

A direct first-hand experience of a scelidosaurus is unlikely in a primary school. The sight of three buses in a row gave one infant class first-hand experience of one aspect of the creature, its length.

In conjunction with a fossil, a shell and a bone, this may establish meaningful connections with living creatures within the children's experience.

An awareness of other times, places and cultures is an important element in the primary school curriculm. Too often the information made available perpetuates over simplifications, stereotypes and over decorated half truths. Illuminating connections can be made with distant experience.

The spice trade, for example is alive and well and on sale at the local supermarket.

SETTING THE SCENE

"It was a difficult matter to persuade me that the tinselled wear upon a hobby-horse was a fine thing. I could not see where was the curiousness or the fineness. Everyone provided objects; but few prepare senses whereby and light wherin to see them."
Thomas Traherne (1636–1674) on his childhood.

Our major learning resource is the classroom.

It has two main functions:

To stimulate or promote learning and equally important, to provide a practical working area with materials and information freely accessible.

Each group of children should come to clearly understand procedures for using, storing, dispensing, replenishing and most important, replacing equipment.

"A classroom should contain, over a period, a wide enough range of resources to provoke the interest of every child, creating the need for him to use and develop his language."
I.L.E.A. Language Guidelines, 1979.

THE TEACHER'S ROLE

To create a rich and stimulating classroom which offers scope for children's curiosity and interest to develop.

To create an all-purpose workshop where learning materials and tools are purposefully organised.

To work alongside the children, sharing and enlarging their experience as well as developing their skills.

To become sensitive to the children's responses and to become more adept at guiding their paths of enquiry. Helping them to recognise new elements and to make new connections for themselves.

To recognise that a simple starting point, from direct first-hand experience has potential for learning across the whole curriculum.

To help children make meaningful decisions and to identify and solve problems (e.g. the appropriate use of tools, information and techniques).

To provide a context in which space, time and resources are available.

"Perception helps talking and talking fixes the grains of perception."

James J. Gibson, The Senses Considered as Perceptual Systems, 1965.

Mrs. Masters

Mrs Masters is the headteacher of the school. Her job is if somebody wants their child to come to the school, she has to take them round. She has to teach the children and she has to see if everything is going right. If somebody is ill she has to telephone their mummy up. She has to organise staff meetings. She also has to make the rules up.

"Language is the mother of thought, not its handmaiden", Karl Kraus, *Half-Truths and One-and-a-Half Truths*, 1930.

TALK

"The school is rightly placing emphasis upon the development of children's talk and command of language as a powerful means of extending learning. Classrooms are being organised to provide environments that offer experiences designed to stimulate children's curiosity and encourage them to pursue varied lines of investigation and study. Staff recognise that language development is largely an interactive process involving children in forms of collaboration calling for discussion, questioning, planning and the collection, evaluation and dissemination of information. Considerable effort is made, therefore, to organise time flexibly to enable children to engage in tasks for extended periods and to facilitate teachers' involvement with groups and individuals.

This process is already yielding valuable consequences. Throughout the school there is opportunity for children to come in contact with and explore, supported by appropriate tools and equipment, wide ranges of objects and forms from the natural world, together with a variety of living creatures and plants. Provision and experience of this kind was richly available in many classes in the second, third and fourth years and, in two cases, outstandingly so. The children's interest and involvement was reflected in increasingly confident use of language. They were competent and enthusiastic about describing what they had done and elaborating on their experiences; they used language effectivly to collaborate with each other and plan future action and they were developing ability to negotiate meaning and to extend awareness through systematic questioning." From an Inspector's Report.

"Observe closely enough," she once said, "and it doesn't matter where you are. You may be in a pitch dark closet. All you want is something to start with; one thing leads to another and all things are mixed up. Shut me up in a dark closet and I will observe after a while, that some places in it are darker than others. After that (give me time), and I will tell you what the President of the United States is going to have for dinner."
Henry James, The Ghostly Rental, 1876.

TABLE TALK—A DRAWING WORKSHOP

This illustration shows a typical "starting point" table prepared for a school-based teachers course.

These "Learning Through Art" courses usually took the form of an introductory slide presentation on The Functions of Art in the Primary School, followed by two further "practical" sessions. One on "Drawing" and one on "Colour".

It says a great deal for the power of tradition that the latter was invariably referred to as "Painting" and teachers sometimes arrived in protective clothing!

As the group usually consisted of the entire staff, representing all stages from Nursery to Top Juniors, the course did not aim to directly relate to current, particular curricular topics. Nor was the intention to present a "Drawing Lesson".

This table was arranged to reflect some of the learning potential of some aspects of the environment. The environment being widely defined as everything outside ourselves, plus ourselves.

It would be appropriate to point out that the objects chosen to introduce a direct experience approach in a class would be indicated by the childrens' own environmental and curricular experience.

Before the course members were asked to select an object to investigate and record, the problems of choosing without criteria for choice were pointed out.

The aspects proposed were shape, structure and the possibility of personal engagement and curiosity.

Attention was focused on the variety of scientific, historic, social and especially linguistic connections that learners might be prompted to make at different stages of skill and awareness.

Thus the emphasis was on looking, questioning and ordering rather than picturing.

Depending on the levels of experience and ability apparent in the group, materials and techniques were offered that tended to increase confidence rather than reinforce timidity. Charcoal was often useful, allowing the less confident teacher to make provisional, tentative marks before reinforcing, altering and refining in the light of increasing knowledge. The simple torn and cut paper print method described towards the end of this book also proved successful with learners who had previously been frustrated by more conventional tools. Any material or technique should allow for the change of intention and the development of ideas that direct experience learning can lead to through an ever widening viewpoint.

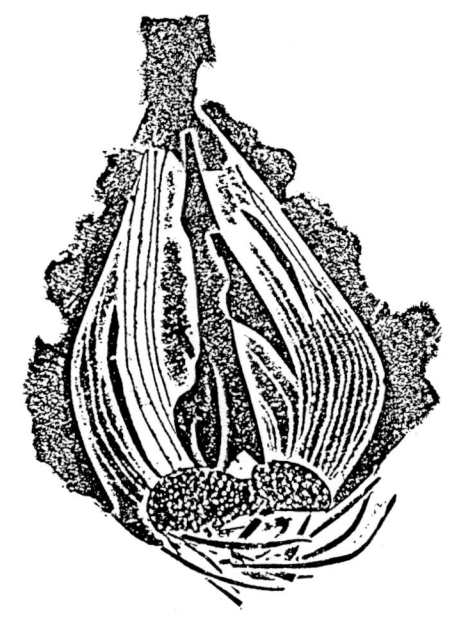

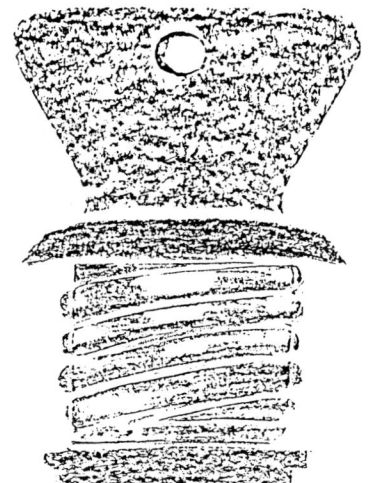

MAKING CONNECTIONS

Although it is undoubtedly helpful to begin with a starting point that can be closely examined and even held in the hand, many vital learning experiences may remain meaningless if their connections, contexts or meanings are left unquestioned. These connections must surely be related to the learner's own perception, language and stages of development.

To examine without curiosity, to record without intention or to reproduce without meaning is . . . meaningless.

"Even if you find many objects and objects that are described in great detail, you will always, and in pride of place, find the eye that considers them and the passion that reshapes them." Alain Robbe-Grillet, Snapshots, 1963.

In a Saturday morning class, a group spent several sessions closely examining and recording insects.

Later in the term, some startling visual parallels were noticed in some of the drawings produced during a session at The Imperial War Museum.

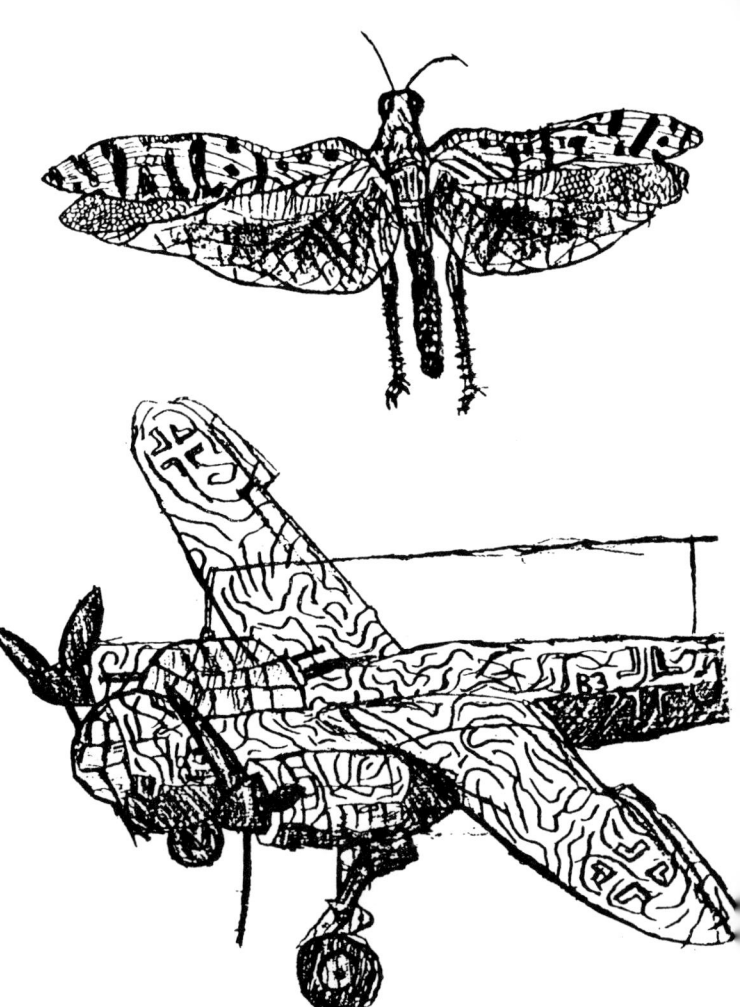

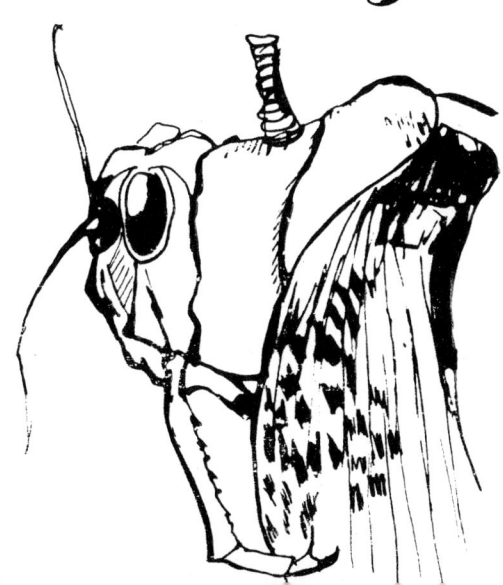

FOCUS

During the early stages of observing, selecting and ordering, questioning is an inseparable part of the activity. Interest and engagement can be shared, communicated and discussed.

What are we looking at?

What are we looking for?

We will want to know how to begin, where to start.

Do we look at the whole shape?

A part?   How large?

How small?

It is always tempting to over direct to superficial solutions rather than lead the children's learning but learners must be enabled to develop their own individual response and interpretation.

Here the teacher becomes a listening, watching co-learner, for new solutions and new problems are being encountered. The magnifying glass has two functions; one of them remains when the lens is removed, it becomes a viewfinder, an aid to focussing, a frame.

"The belief that science proceeds from observation to theory is still so widely and so firmly held that my denial of it is often met with incredulity. I have even been suspected of being insincere, of denying what nobody in his senses can doubt. But in fact the belief that we can start with pure observations alone, without anything in the nature of a theory, is absurd. Observation is always selective. It needs a chosen object, a definite task, an interest, a point of view, a problem. And its description presupposes interests, points of view and problems."
Karl Popper, Conjectures and Refutations, 1986.

DRAWING AN OBJECT

There is a natural progression for the learner from the examination of a single, isolated object.

Drawing an object in a secure and comfortable environment helps to focus research whilst confidence and skills are gained. These activities involving seeing as well as recording skills, help to develop the learner's ability to order their response to direct experience.

This can lead to learners encountering the need to extend their understanding and further refine the personal qualities of their responses to a learning situation.

It takes time, practice, skill and confidence to scan or read even a simple object and learn more from it.

It is worth remembering, that however "self-contained" the object may be, it is in fact part of the environment to which we all belong.

"Just as the artist is greatly helped by an exact knowledge of the separate parts of the human figure which he must finally regard as a whole, so a general view and a glance at related objects is a great advantage, so long as the artist is capable of rising to ideas and of grasping the close relationships of things apparently remote.
  Comparitive anatomy has prepared a general concept of organic nature; it leads us from form to form, and by observing organisms closely or distantly related, we rise above them to see their characteristics in an ideal picture."
J. W. von Goethe. On Art, 1772.

The common scaffolding clip, studied in the classroom reveals some of its function. When seen in context, equally common, its purpose is further understood.

TEACHERS AS LEARNERS

This programme gives some indication of the aims and scope of a series of "Learning Through Art" courses.

They were designed for non-specialist primary school teachers who were able to be released for one week during term time. The courses sought, not to provide "Tips for Teachers", but attempted to guide teachers at all stages of primary learning, towards developing their confidence and skills.

The course base was a spare classroom rather than an Art studio. It contained, as well as basic materials, a variety of possible starting points and reference material. Its situation in London's dockland gave added interest and opportunities.

For many of the teacher/learners, the most valuable aspect was the opportunity to become familiar, away from classroom pressures, with basic materials and processes which, in many cases, they had found discouraging during their own brief art education.

The course members particularly appreciated the time to review and question their own philosophy and practice in this area of the curriculum

This may well be the most essential ingredient in any in-service programme
When initial uncertainties and concern with end products had been diffused, the simple "learning to look" exercises developed into more personal responses. Individual decision making became possible.

LEARNING THROUGH ART
ST. PATRICK'S WAPPING

Course Organisers: Maurice Rubens
                   Mary Newland

Sessions: Monday - Friday, 9.30-16.00 hours

A mainly practical course with special emphasis on drawing and painting as a vehicle for learning. The basic elements of Art will be studied in relation to observing, recording and communicating. The importance of first-hand experience will be stressed throughout this course.

Introduction
Encountering the learner's needs.
Visual stimulus as a starting point for learning.
Learning to look - looking to learn.
Drawing as investigation - de-mystifying drawing.
Child development and Art Across the Curriculum slide talk.
Extending drawing, mark making, decision making, recording, prolonging looking.
Graphic materials and tools examined.
Colour and the visible curriculum.
Analytical and personal response to the environment - defining areas of investigation.
Personal extension, making cross curricular connections.
Evaluation and display as extended learning.

Towards the end of the week, teachers were encouraged to develop strategies, based on their own learning experience, that would enable them to extend their particular curricular interests when they returned, the following Monday, to the "real world".

Follow Up

As well as the basic course, Head Teacher's courses, Induction courses and Extending courses were provided.

With only two advisory teachers responsible for the courses as well as Art across the curriculum in a large authority's 800 primary schools, follow up was patchy.

Where possible, teachers were visited and given support. In many cases, one or more 'course graduates' initiated school based workshops in their own schools.

Aspects of one of these courses are described elsewhere in this book.

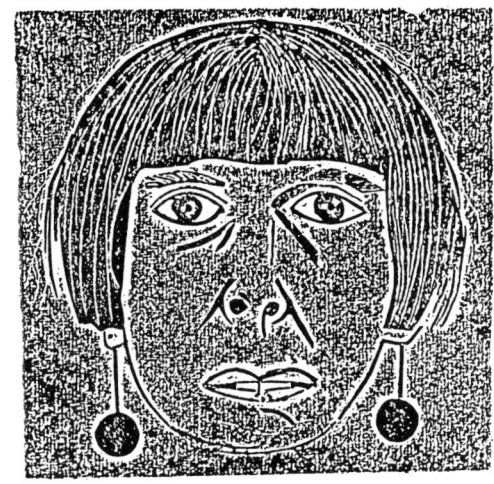

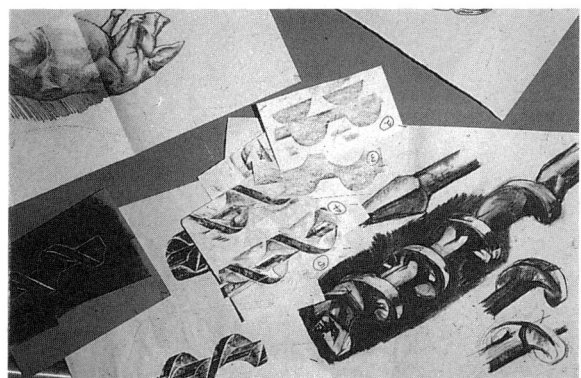

SEEING AND THINKING

Holes caves and columns.

The holding arm of a mother and child sculpture. One finds forms of great strength contrasting with others of amazing delicacy.
With more complexity than there is in a human skull.

Vertical and horizontal form.

Skull side view eye socket and tusk holes.

Skull side view jaw articulation.

Bones have great variety in section and subtle transition of one shape into another.

Bones have marvellous structural strength and hard tenseness of form.

Illusionist drawing-linear technique.

Here I was searching for the skull's internal structure. Though still only a line drawing I wanted to show the skull's massiveness.

Rocks arch and tunnel.

The elephant is the most remarkable living link we have with the prehistoric world.

Head of a cyclops.

One form cupped and socketed into another.

Doric columns and underground dungeons.

Elephant Skull (Detail) Henry Moore

...sed the hairlike fineness of line to suggest space and
...ystery.

...esert sandhills stretching to the horizon.

...s the most impressive item in my library of natural forms.

...ew of a female back.

...vo interlocking figures.

... competing this drawing I thought of Piranesi's series of
...aginary prisons.

...ew of a male torso.

...ull's back view tunnels regressions dark depths.

...enry Moore's thoughts whilst drawing an elephant's skull)

Prisons (Detail) Giam Battista Piranesi.

DRAWING A MARROW IN A PRIMARY SCHOOL

It needs a big piece of paper.

It will take a long time to draw.

It's like a balloon. What's inside?

How old is it? How do they grow?

Can you eat it? Does it smell?

It looks splashed.

You get lost looking at the yellow dots.

It's like a giant nut. Can we open it?

The stalk looks like a handle on my wardrobe.

When you spit on the crayon it smudges like the marrow.

The yellow marks run into each other like rain on the window.

It would be better to paint it.

The drawings were too big and colourful to reproduce in this book. (That was not their purpose!) so let's look at more elephants . . .

"The elephant has been adopted as the emblem of one of our great political parties for a number of reasons. It has a sagacious profile and a cunning eye and its loose skin and paunch suggest the clothing and figure of some of our well-known politicians of bygone days . . . yet there is about the movement of this greatest of living mammals remarkable grace and rhythm; study the elephant, if the opportunity presents itself. You will find it a fascinating subject and perhaps, a far more beautiful one than you at first realised."
Alexander Calder whose wire sculpture is illustrated.

The success of the elephant, as opposed to fluffier, furrier creatures, is surprising. Laurent de Brunhoff, creator of Babar and Celeste, thought that elephants, being fat and slow moving are reassuring to children. Certainly, there can be no mother on earth more reassuring than Celeste.

"Great importance was placed on naturalism in the making of Dumbo. Special art classes – an extension of the existing training programme – were instituted so that Rico Lebrun could instruct the animators in the finer points of drawing animals. An elephant was kept on the lot as a model for the artists. Books of photographic studies and innumerable model sheets were compiled, along with analyses of animal action and thousands of feet of live action material to be used for reference."
Walt Disney.

THE JUNGLE PROJECT

This 4th year junior class was able to have the use for one day of a classroom in a college of higher education.

On arrival the children were introduced to a variety of natural objects found in the college grounds.

Through discussion they were able to relate the objects to the visible landscape (the room was glazed on three sides).

Visual qualities they identified were related to the linear and tonal qualities of charcoal.

The initial drawing led to the need for an understanding of a third element, scale.

Fragments were considerably enlarged and a wider range of mark-making developed.

After a break for an indoor picnic lunch, the class took charcoal, large white brushwork paper and drawing boards into the nearby Winter Garden, a large Edwardian greenhouse full of sub-tropical plants and trees.

The children were asked to use their experience of charcoal and mark-making to respond to and record the particular unreal though certainly "in-Eltham" atmosphere.

They encountered initial difficulties in selecting and ordering their drawing, but with some guidance and help from simple card viewfinders they began to come to terms with the problems of making sense of the profusion bordering on confusion of the architecture as well as the plants themselves.

Alongside this "Art-based" activity the class were also involved in other areas of the curriculum.

Reference materials that were needed included books which enabled identification, classification and understanding of the plants, historical and architectural information on the Winter Garden, the geographic origins of some plants and scientific data on plant and animal conservation.

A further dimension was added by the chance discovery of the work of the painter Henri Rousseau (1844–1910).

Second and third (school-based) sessions.

These half-days in the classes' own base introduced some of the functions of colour through the medium of chalk pastels, after some research and colour mixing tests.

The work on location and some reproductions of the work of Rousseau, who painted jungles in Paris, using his experience of winter gardens and picture books, led to forest and jungle pictures.

These pictures used, in addition to the children's notes, some plastic animals and the range of pot-plants in the classroom.

These tools, materials and skills were further developed when applied to a class project on "People".

This demanded other levels of precision and sensitivity, particularly when it led to self-portraits.

see pages -7 -25 -42

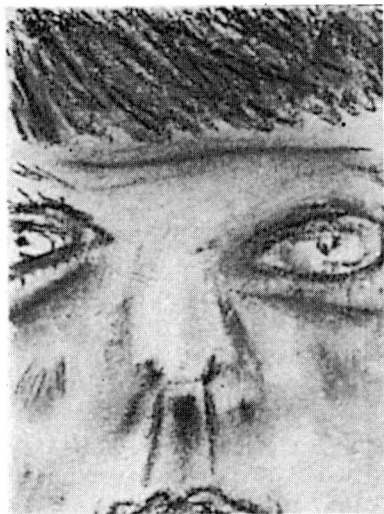

MAKING MEANING

"The purpose of Art is to close the gap between you and everything that is not you and thus proceed from feeling to meaning." Robert Hughes, The Shock of the New, 1982.

Drawing keeps the eye engaged and is an excellent starting point for deciphering an unfamiliar phenomenom.

Some images lose some or all of their meaning without colour. Some meanings are coveyed by shape and structure. Communicating meaning depends on some common language. Writing is an abstract language that serves function. Visual art can sometimes communicate more directly. An intelligible sign in its proper context may be no more than a white line painted on a road. The symbolic elements of a sign language owe their intelligibility to our recognition of what they represent.

Signs and symbols must therefore evolve from common, direct experience.

To reproduce without meaning is meaningless. So much truth exists that it is barely necessary to invent any.

"I may live in an age of photography and films, but what I do could not be photographed, because I don't in fact copy objects. Instead I observe an object and then regurgitate it. It has passed through the 'sausage mincer' of my consciousness. If that is interesting then it acquires interest."
Erich Brauer.

"We often talk as though ideas become expressed in material form. This is misleading.

"Idea is made in the interaction between the individual's feeling experienced as impulse for release, and the medium which he works into the form that releases it."
Robert Witkin, The Intelligence of Feeling, 1974.

SOME INTENTIONS OR WHY BEFORE HOW

Confusion in the mind of the teacher and the learner as to the intentions of a piece of work can be avoided by not only defining an area of study, perhaps limiting its initial scope, but by attempting to more closely relate enquiry to the learner's perceived needs.

Removing pressure on the learner to produce a quick and decorative end product will probably increase security and lead to real exploration.

"He had an amazing ability to get inside the mind of the student, to become a critic from within the person. He was in no way dogmatic and would question not what they were doing, but why. Why before How ruthlessly stripped away the pretentiousness that an art school environment can encourage, and Hans would gently redirect his students to face themselves as their own prime critics."
Tony Birks on Hans Coper.

"There was a basic need for a book that told you not only how but why—why mustn't you add the egg quickly so it doesn't curdle? Why should you seal meat? Why mustn't you over beat the egg-whites?"
Delia Smith. The Other Hunger, 1981.

"A fanatic is one who redoubles his effort when he has forgotten his aim." George Santayana, The Last Puritan, 1940.

Drawings by girl, 7, which trapped rapist
These are the sketches coaxed from a rape victim, aged seven, which led to the arrest of her attacker 30 hours after the ordeal.
The girl was given crayons and a sketch pad by WPC Liz ...

These diagrammatic drawings, although not made in a school context, underline the way drawing may be able to communicate when other language is not available or appropriate.

LOOKING AT ART

What is its aim or intention?
Does it contain one or more levels of meaning?

What is its function?
Is it a direct response to an experience?

What is its visual language or imagery?
Is it an invented, adapted, or imaginary response?

What is its idea?

What style is it in?
Is its main or only aim to decorate, demonstrate, or illustrate?

What is it made of?

When was it made?
How is it made?

What is its context?
Historical? Literary? Religious? Psychological? Social? Scientific?

In what circumstances was it conceived and created?

For whom was it created?
What did the artist hope to achieve?

What means did he employ?
Conscious or unconscious?

Did the artist succeed?

Do existing preparatory drawings or studies give us insight into the creative process?
Do sources include recall of experience, use of reference materials or models?

Does the work of other artists on similar themes help us to understand the artist's problems and ambitions?

What can we learn from an examination of the artist's handling of materials?

What is the work's impact on its contemporaries?

What are the implications for the further development of the artist's ideas?
What are the implications for the further development of our ideas?

By examining a work of art and focusing on aspects of its creation, knowledge and understanding of artists and our world is increased.

LOOKING AT CHILDREN'S WORK

What is its aim or intention?
What is its function?

What is its idea?
The child's, the teacher's, another's?

What is it made from?

How is it made?
Are the materials and methods appropriate? (to the subject, to the child's stage of development?) Does it promote learning?

How was it made?
Slowly? Quickly?

Where was it made?
In a lesson? In an Art lesson? Elsewhere?

Why was it made?
Does it contain one or more levels of meaning?

What is its context?
Historical? Social? Literary? Scientific?

How old or at what stage of development is the child?

Does it reflect the child's ideas or the child's response to the ideas of others?

How does it relate to the work of other children, other artists?
For whom was it created?

How does it relate to the overall learning experience of the child?
*What did the child hope to achieve?
What did the teacher hope to achieve?
What means were employed?
Do sources include recall of experience, use of reference or models?
Conscious or Unconscious?*

Did the child succeed?

Does the work relate to previous work in this or other areas of learning?
*Does the way other children have dealt with these problems help us to understand the child's problems and ambitions?
Was the choice and handling of materials appropriate and successful?
What is the reaction of the child and of other children to the work?*

What are the implications for the further development in this and other areas of learning?
By examining the work of a child and focusing on aspects of its creation our knowledge and understanding of our world is increased.

These drawings, made at home by a seven year old used extensive research in a personal collection of pony literature.

CONTEXT AND FUNCTION

The size and scale of work is often part of its meaning. Tentatively recording the first response is often the first step to understanding and discovering a personal meaning. What is already known will help to define what is to be found. Other learners' questions are often as relevant as our own. The daily life of a classroom will cross fertilise any project.

"We never look at just one thing: We are always looking at the relation between things and ourselves."
John Berger, Ways of Seeing, 1972.

This middle-junior school work was initiated by a teacher bringing his father's toy trains to the classroom. The cut paper prints of track required investigation into their construction as well as accurate measurement.

BEYOND THE CLASSROOM

A well furnished classroom usually contains a wide range of resources, rare as well as familiar. These should help to interest and engage each learner in relation to every stage of development, in all areas of the curriculum.

However much a classroom reflects the learner's experience of the world, it is bound to be limited.

The learner's growing awareness demands a broader viewpoint and a range of "off-site" experiences should be incorporated into each term's learning.

"If we look back at our schooldays, what were the moments when something really important and memorable happened? And where were you when it happened? In the classroom? Doubtful."
Harry Ree, Are Schools the Enemy? 1981.

SOME LEARNING LOCATIONS

Hand . . . Table-top . . . Cupboard . . . Window ledge . . . Corridor . . . Hall . . . Playground . . . Street . . . Park . . . Bus stop . . . Shops . . . Church . . . House . . . Garden . . . Roof-top . . . Building site . . . Sports Centre . . . Hospital . . . Fête . . . Concert . . . Fire Station . . . Canal . . . Town Hall . . . Rivers . . . Bridges . . . Railways . . . City Farms . . . Zoos . . . Docks . . . Historical sites . . . Castles . . . Palaces . . . Museums . . . Art Galleries . . . Theatres . . . School Journeys . . . . and Supermarkets . . . .

Vincent van Gogh found it helpful to look at the outside world from the safe enclosure of a window.

When he came to work outdoors he said it made him dizzy. He asked a carpenter to construct a frame that would stand up without walls.

The use of this frame gave him the feeling of observing nature from a sheltered, secure viewpoint. The drawing describing the construction of this device survives in a letter.

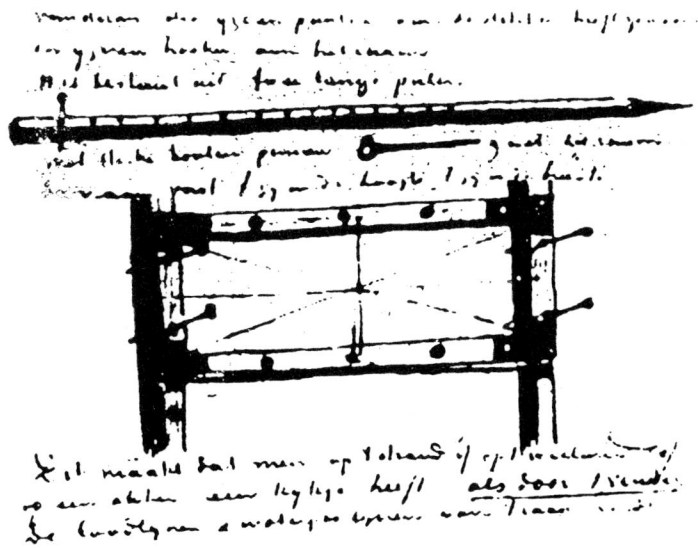

LEARNING ON LOCATION

Drawing on location needs careful preparation and planning. The teacher must know some of the aims and objectives of such activity. The teacher must act as a catalyst, continually reseaching new and appropriate areas, near or far for learning excursions. The teacher must always make preliminary visits to the site and become familiar with the special qualities and characteristics that will interest and engage the children.

It is not always necessary to work far from the school building. Often a rich and stimulating environment is to be found near by. Inner city schools are situated in a remarkably wide range of neighbourhoods, from recent housing estates and Georgian squares to street markets and docks.

Some schools possess a roof-top playground with a splendid view of infinite variety, others overlook gardens or factories.

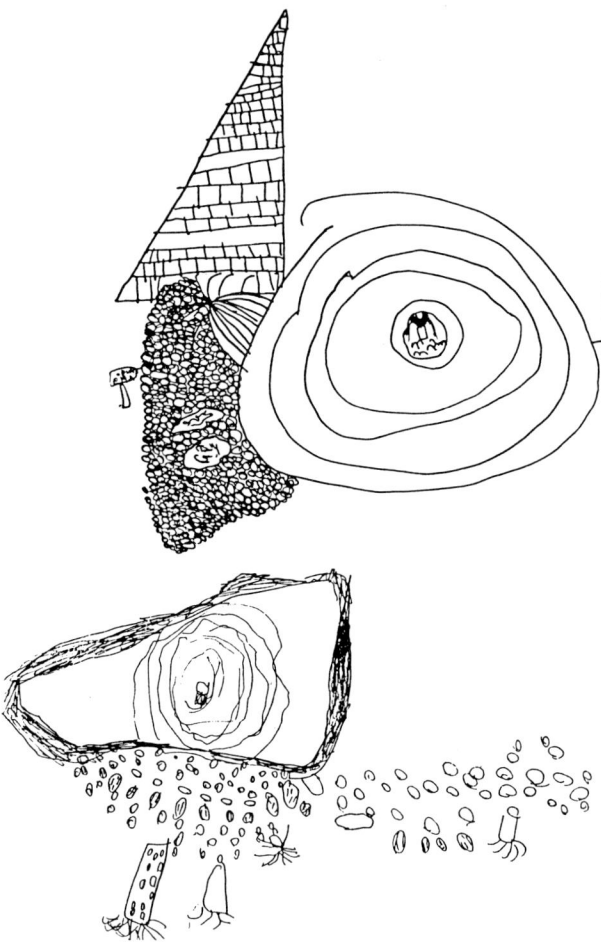

These drawings were made by infants on location at Kew Gardens. The paintings were made in school using the drawings and other reference material (books, plants, conversation).

Infants at Westminster

Nursery *Infants and Juniors look at the church next-door*

BEFORE WE GO...SOME AIMS

Before leaving the classroom, teachers and learners should have some clear intentions, some skills, some questions.

To encounter real things e.g. Buildings, animals, machinery, people, trees etc. for the rewards of understanding and perhaps recording something well, or to find experience unobtainable in school.

To discover and examine aspects of our environment. And to study them, perhaps by isolating the visual (and other) elements, e.g. the shapes, colours, textures materials, structures and **purposes** of a wall.

To draw for particular information required for a project. Often these records can be reinforced by written notes, e.g. studying a working crane in order to construct a scientific model.

To experience our world at first-hand. e.g. aspects of history, geography or science studied in areas like St Katherine's Dock.

Before taking children out to draw on location it is essential they have already encountered the challenges of drawing from direct experience in the classroom situation.

Children will find drawing outside the school environment a demanding task.

They will have to come to terms with physical difficulties, the size and scale of the world outside and the selection of an appropriate area for study.

Comfort plays an important part in the achievement of successful location learning.

The children need to work on a flat, firm surface, to be able to sit comfortably and have a clear viewpoint.

In most instances, materials should be distributed to children before leaving the classroom.

They can then be responsible for their own equipment.

A drawing board can be improvised from hardboard or a strong strawboard.

Paper can be carefully stapled or held firmly with masking tape.

A strong bulldog clip (why so called?) converts the board into a handy clipboard.

A group of juniors spent an afternoon drawing their local Health Centre, seen from the front garden of their school. They were later involved with the publication of the Centre's brochure which used their drawings as illustrations.

FOCUSING SELECTING QUESTIONING

Even with the confidence and skills acquired in the classroom, once on location the learners will need help in focusing and selecting an area to be studied.

During the process of selecting, questioning is an inseparable part of the activity.

This questioning will only be productive if both the teacher and the learner are on the way to an understanding of their intentions. The informal but structured neighbourhood exploration can become a regular part of learning practice across the curriculum. Every school offers within its immediate environment, stimulation, motivation and the possibility of active engagement for the developing child; but an even wider range of learning opportunities can be found further afield.

School journeys and well organised gallery and museum visits provide firsthand experience beyond the everyday, known local environment.

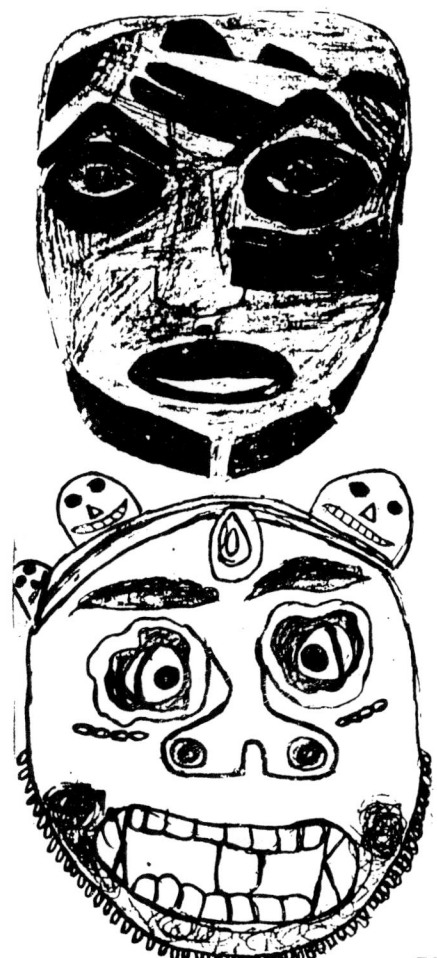

Juniors at The Horniman Museum

FINDING OUR WAY

Zoos, farms, museums, galleries or even reference libraries are not primarily designed to be easily accessible to the enquiring child. (Though many are now offering educational programmes.) It is sometimes easy to overlook the extra dimensions of the unknown, often forbidding, that can be encountered in a new environment.

Lighting, labelling, frames, glass cases, scale, size and above all quantity can overwhelm, frighten, frustrate and discourage.

Both learner and teacher can be lost in a situation that is not always designed in the best interests of the learner.

No one was able to give us a figure for the number of objects in The British Museum but a spokesperson at The Tate Gallery said 6,000 objects were catalogued.

"Because I don't know what it is, I can't look at it."
Overheard in The Victoria and Albert Museum.

This drawing represents some of the excitement a group of infants experienced during a visit to The London Toy and Model Museum. Back at school they went on to examine, in words and pictures more personal aspects of toys.

Yesterday on Tuesday October the fourth my class went to the London Toy Museum and one of my favourite things were the carousel and a train that went across a track that you can ride on. that had a crocodile in the water but it was pretend and it was made of stone and in the middle of the coach outside there was another crocodile that was on hard ground. In front of the old coach there was a shed so it could not move. In the shop I liked the inflatable Aeroplane.

"My Russian doll came from Russia. My Auntie went to Russia and she went into a shop and she saw a Russian doll and she bought it for me and I was five and the doll is seven I say. I brought it into school because we were drawing our toys and I brought it in because I like it."

(The illustration has been assisted by a photo-copying session which produced a more acute awareness of size and scale as well as some surprising infant observations as to individual dolls' variety of detail.)

LOOKING AND SEEING

During a museum or gallery visit the chief aim should be for the children to see the object clearly for themselves, without interfering with a partly formulated but growing, personal, visual and possibly emotional response.

As teachers we must try to ensure that any factual, historical, scientific, social or other information is presented in ways that relate to both previous experience and to whatever is seen by looking.

Both comfort and clarity must play a part in choosing an area for study.

PREPARATION

All tools and materials including reference and recording material should be both familiar and available before and after the visit if the work is to provide potential for further development in other areas of learning.

Often, even a short trip requires so much time and preparation that its value is minimal unless those involved are adequately equipped on their return with sufficient information, reference material, knowledge and confidence to be able to extend and develop their researches in the classroom.

These materials might include:
Drawing and other notes; painting and colour notes; photographs; measurements; rubbings; maps; tape recordings; postcards; books; leaflets; found objects (that can be re-examined) and memories.

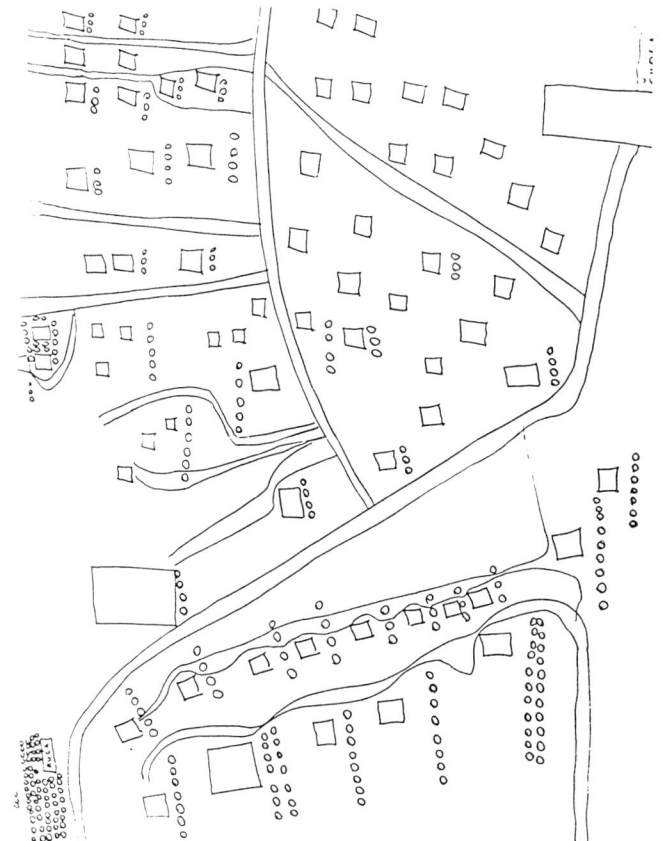

"When I work outside, I like painting the shapes accurately and getting the shadows right . . . but it is difficult to get everything to the right proportion because the world is so large."
Giles, I.L.E.A. Saturday classes.

DO WE HAVE TO DRAW?

Although the main emphasis in this book is on drawing from direct experience as a way of learning in the primary school, a well prepared visit to the museum, an art gallery or an exhibition can be developed in other valuable directions.

Many galleries and museums have education departments whose aim is to extend the experience of teachers and learners. Most education departments offer practical assistance to teachers planning visits.

Talks, information sheets and in some cases, a workroom are among the facilities available. Preliminary enquiries are particularly welcomed.

Some galleries and museums have recently begun to offer courses, workshops and open evenings especially for teachers. The question at the head of this page, has however, wider implications, Drawing, in some form has occupied a place in the curriculum from the earliest days of formal education.

"It being the opinion of all present that the art of drawing is absolutely necessary in many employments, trades and manufactures and that encouragement thereof may prove of great utility to the public."

(Meeting of noblemen, clergymen, gentlemen and merchants in Rawthmills Coffee House, March 1754 to found a society for the encouragement of Arts, Manufacture and Commerce in Great Britain.)

"We must call into play the intellectual powers of the pupils. Drawing has been too long regarded by schoolmasters and schoolmistresses as a mere mechanical art."
T. R. Ablett. How to Teach Drawing in Elementary Schools, 1889.

"In spite of his strength and activity I think Charles must always have had a clumsiness of movement. He was naturally awkward and was unable to draw at all well. This he always regretted ('an irremediable evil') and frequently urged the paramount necessity of a young naturalist making himself a good draughtsman."
Francis Darwin, Life and Letters of Charles Darwin, 1890.

AN HISTORICAL PERSPECTIVE

From earliest times, education systems have usually made some provision for the inclusion of drawing.

Here, about 1906, we see the newly discovered phenomenom, "the child". Although still dressed as small adults, they are involved in a drawing activity.

About thirty years later this activity was banished from most curricula.

Before we look at its replacement, let us examine its credentials.

It is said to train hand and eye, encouraging observation and memory. It promotes an awareness of nature's beauty. Even more significantly drawing can record, plan, investigate and develop design. (The first Art and Design colleges, set up on 1851 Exhibition profits were called Drawing Schools.) A thoughtful teacher might regret that any learning produced under the conditions shown here will have ended the day wiped out by a wet cloth. This would lose the capacity for further learning gained by a learner with the competence and confidence to record their learning. One might also question the implied assumption of an entire class at the same developmental stage.

These factors, however, were not the ones considered when, 30 years later, a newly discovered phenomenom became prominent, "The Child Artist".

"Children," we were told, "have a way of communicating that is uniquely their own, for they have not been sophisticated by adult standards and are uncluttered by the cultural conventions of the society in which they are growing up."

"Leave them alone and don't interfere with their individual free expression," became the rule. Another tenet of this system of child art production, for such it is, was the dubious belief that small hands can better control and manipulate giant-size brushes, extravagantly fluid, garish paint. (They love bright colours!) and crayons designed to mark large packing crates. This abdication of the teacher's instructional role has led to several generations of learners who, having not surprisingly failed to express anything without a language, have grown up visually illiterate.

Further confusion and frustration is caused by indiscriminate and evaluation free adoration of the "Art" thus produced. Children who cannot or will not conform to the accepted formula are seen, however tactfully, as un-talented failures and are thereby diverted from developing some of their most valuable learning skills.

Marion Richardson (LCC Inspector) wrote to London Headteachers soliciting pictures for a Jubilee Exhibition of The New Art Teaching in 1935. She added a postscript requesting a few examples of "The old way" as contrast.

Since that jubilee (the exhibition was visited by the two little princesses), changes and innovations have proliferated. Most of them notable for more vigour than rigour.

Experiment, Exploration and Interesting Materials are but three that heralded the current era of the closely observed teasel. An experiment as a test without hypothesis is akin to the explorer without maps, map-reading or map-making skills. When the Royal Navy rescue party arrive, they will have another name for him.

String, wire, foil, beans and cardboard cartons require at least as much manipulative skill as simpler, direct materials. The unquestioned acceptance of these approaches has led the less confident teacher to over direct in order to fulfil the end product quota. This leads to the destruction of the qualities of individuality the approach claims to foster. When basic materials become tools for learning from direct experience we can consider extending provision for identifiable needs.

The approaches proposed in this book must not be read as a plea for a return to Victorian values. The drawings of daffodils, based as they seem to be on the belief that there is one correct way of drawing that plant, regardless of function, need or other experience, can only be of limited value. The picture of the boy with a clipboard in a museum might at first sight, be read as modern dress revisionism. Are the stuffed birds proposed as innately superior to daffodils? Is he in fact drawing? The birds? Parts of them? He might, (for photography has not advanced so much in 80 years), be writing, prose or verse, engaged in geographic, historic or mathematic enquiry. He may even be preparing a reflected self-portrait. What he is engaged in depends on him. His previous experience, his present skills and his needs. The Bullock Report, dealing with Language in the Early Years, emphasised the need to create;

"Situations in which to satisfy his own purposes, a child encounters the need to use more elaborate forms, and is thus motivated to extend the complexity of language available to him."

This proposal, purged perhaps of the sexist pronouns of 1974, might provide a basic bench-mark/guideline to help teachers to promote situations providing stimulation, motivation and active engagement.

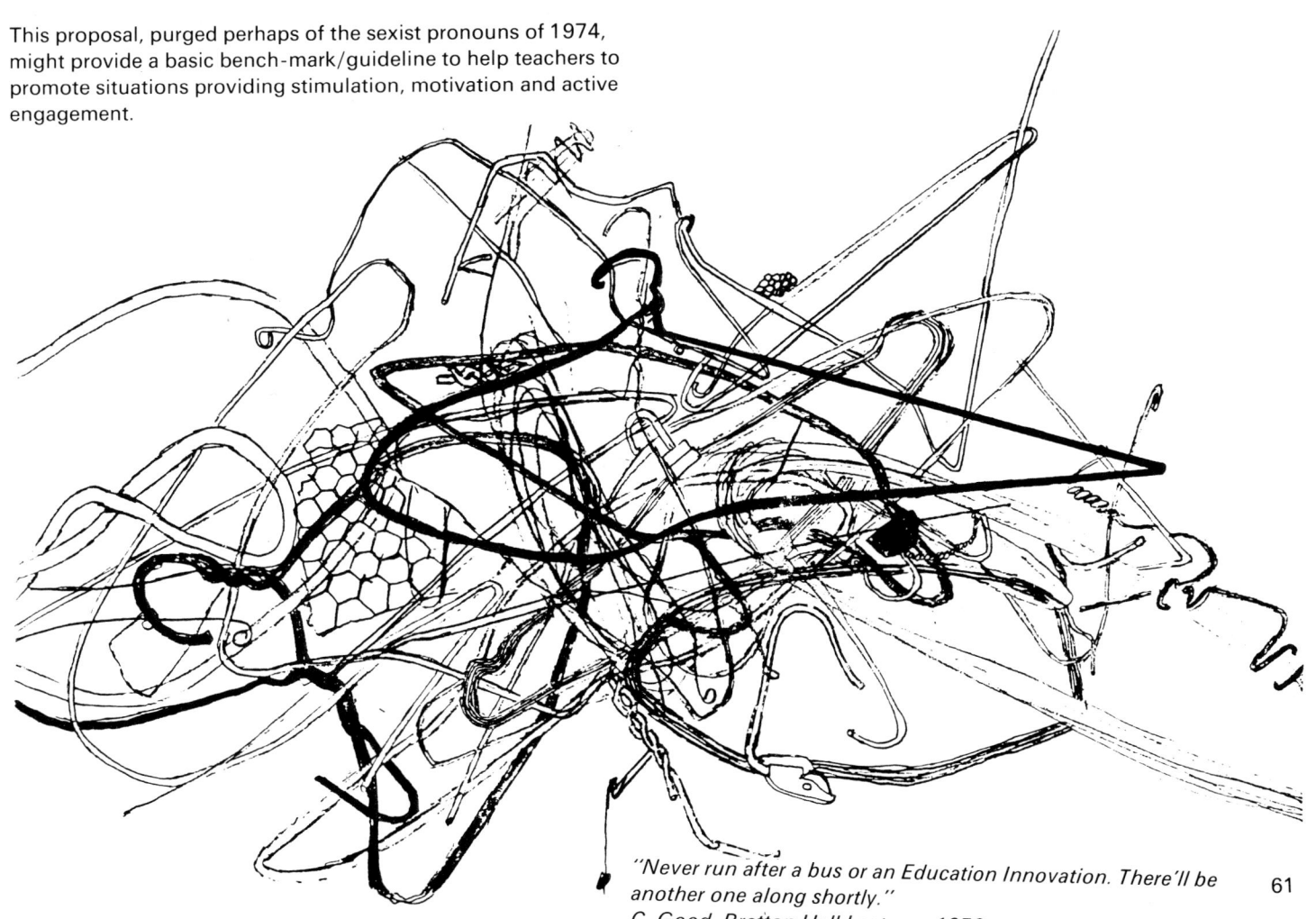

"Never run after a bus or an Education Innovation. There'll be another one along shortly."
C. Good, Bretton Hall Lecturer, 1956.

TOOLS

At this point, having glanced at where we have come from in order to arrive where we are (surely a prerequisite to going anywhere), we might literally "Take stock" and look at some of the basic tools and materials we need.

The next pages, more usually expected at the end of a publication, should never be taken for granted.

The teacher needs to acquire a reservoir of experience to be able to advise and guide the learner towards the appropriate means.

GRAPHIC MATERIALS

A vast range of visual experiences can be absorbed and understood through looking at shape and structure before colour becomes essential. Learners can be helped to use drawing as a means of discovery. A process to assist learning.

Charcoal. Is often seen as a sort of poor relation who must be hidden away when brightly coloured visitors arrive. Charcoal marks are not final or decisive until we fix them. (Cheap non-CVC hair lacquer is as good as a fixative and has the added bonus of perfume!) The character of charcoal marks allows a drawn response to be modified and adjusted in the light of learning.

Pencils. Especially soft ones, B, 2B, 3B and those thick ones called beginners or starters can be seen as versatile tools producing a great variety of lines, marks and tones. It is necessary to allow time to become familiar with the particular properties of any tool. This is especially true of the pencil if the learner is not to be discouraged by confusing what has been learned about writing tools with needs to produce other marks.

Ink. Makes decisive marks calling for some premeditation. The demands of a fine pen will promote a careful and constructive attitude to a drawing's gradual development. Self-made bamboo pens (garden sticks) encourage sensitive awareness of the individual, expressive nature of marks. Ink may also be used with brushes and its tonal range expanded with water.

Ball point pens and Fibre-tip pens. In a range of thicknesses are fine for working away from the classroom base. Reproductions of other learners' (artists) uses of drawing materials are indispensable.

SHALL I COLOUR IT IN?

Some images lose some or all of their meaning without colour, while some meanings are conveyed by shape and structure alone. We must try to avoid the situation whereby meaning is obliterated by the addition of colour.

This might suggest that more than one piece of work is sometimes needed to fully express a response to experience. The child's response to experience will ultimately include the positive need to use colour.

When this need arises, the appropriate colour must be available. From the earliest stages, learners must be given the opportunity to make controlled, considered and tentative statements in response to their experience of colour.

Teachers and learners can share the research and exploration of materials and the shared discovery of each materials appropriate function.

Whatever colour is used, its organisation, storage and distribution should cause no disruption to the functioning of the school and the promotion of learning.

However the teacher arranges the provision in the classroom, the aim should be for individuals, groups or classes to have access to appropriate means whenever a learning situation demands colour. If this can be achieved without mop-buckets, blocked sinks, dry-cleaning or protective clothing the educational gains are enormous.

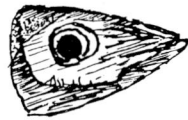

Drawing with pen, brush and ink.

PAINT IN THE CLASSROOM

Powder paint is probably the most common colour medium used in primary schools. It seems to have become established when there were few cheap alternatives. Its storage, accessibility and use can create problems. Particularly in a general classroom situation which rarely allows for a special art area. It is indisputable that an experience of mixing colour from a dry powder is educational. Unfortunately, this necessary process often distracts the learner from the directness and immediacy of a response to colour.

It has been our classroom experience, over many years, that the most practical, fluid and economical direct colour experience can be provided by large, dry colour blocks. These, in an imperfect world are as near as possible, to trouble-free colour. With a little practice, they allow dense or transparent, mixed and matched colours to be achieved over a wide range of scales and sizes.

Ready mixed paint, supplied in plastic bottles (stored in a wine-rack and monitored and shaken from time to time), might be considered as a useful alternative/supplement. If they are provided in the suggested, basic colour range, the procedure should be for each child to set out a palette at the start of the session. If very small "toothpaste" quantities are carefully squeezed on to a palette that has spare accommodation for mixtures, the amount wasted in washing-up is minimal.

For exceptional work when large quantities of generalised colour are needed for stage scenery or large posters, powder paint is the most economical. Science, maths and hygiene can here be brought to bear on the problems that will be encountered.

A range of brushes

Fitches, hog hair

No 4   No 6   No 8   No 10   No 16

Sable, Synthetic Sable

No 4   No 6   No 7

Filbert hog hair

No 3   No 6

"Those whose feelings are unintelligible to them are as assuredly handicapped in the regulating of their lives as those who are unable to think coherently and can make little sense the world they share with other men."
Robert Witkin, The Intelligence of Feeling, 1974.

Quack quack, the ducklings go
Calling for their mothers
Crying in its language "Let me go home"
The farmer shows no pity on the ducklings
He throws them in a cardboard box
I picked one out of the box and started to rub it
With my hand on its soft fur
It clinches on to my neck by its beak
And starts to go to sleep
But then I had to put it back in its box
It tried to get out but did not succeed
And had to go to another home.

SOME MATERIALS

Dry colour materials are capable of a great range of visual refinement. *Coloured pencil-crayons* are more blendable if used on white cartridge paper.

Chalk pastel-crayons. Like charcoal are often poorly regarded. This is partly due to their commonly overcrowded living conditions. If sets of colours are stored in separate containers they can be more clearly understood and used for a wide range of finely controlled work with colour.

Paint. There are many aspects of experience and learning that not only demand colour for their expression and understanding but also require the particular, fluid qualities of paint. Whether powder colour, tempera block paint or ready mixed paint is used a basic range of colours is essential. A suggested range of basic colours is shown here . . . .

Palettes, for controlled mixing and an understanding of their use as a basic tool, should be seen as essential training in the use of the classroom as a resource.

Although these materials have traditionally been used by artists and children at different stages of development they should be re-introduced gradually and their usage explored and extended in connection with learning experiences that their particular qualities can enhance.

"Experience is my true mistress."
Leonardo da Vinci, 1452–1519.

"Limitation of means determines style, engenders new forms and gives impulse to creation."
George Braque, Notebooks, 1917–1955.

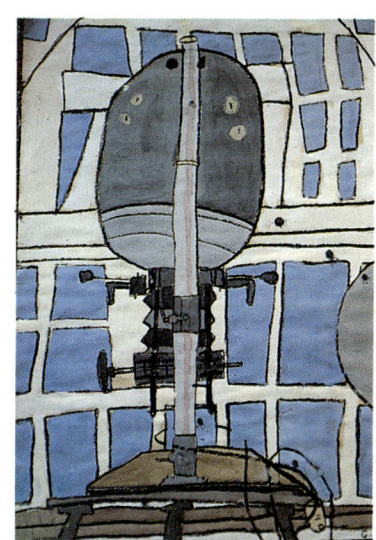

(A suggested range of primary colours is shown here.)

  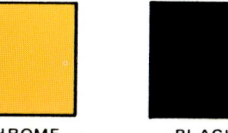 

VERMILION RED   COBALT BLUE   CHROME YELLOW   BLACK

CRIMSON   PRUSSIAN or CYAN BLUE   LEMON YELLOW   WHITE

EXPRESSION

During the primary school years, a child begins to move from an early self-centredness and becomes increasingly aware of and sensitive to the viewpoints, capabilities and opinions of others.

Connections are discovered and comparisons made. Across the curriculum, the relationship of parts to the whole and size to scale becomes important.

Encountering demands and needs with a growing vocabulary of skills including language, the child wishes to share a view, and not only to share it, but to get it "right".

Whose answers are sought?

If the early years have been put to good use and have expanded enquiry skills as well as confidence with tools, the child will be ready to make personal statements founded on first hand experience. These, not only of the material world but reflecting the individual's inner response to being alive.

This is the foundation of expression, whether of reality or what we chose to call fantasy.

Reality is no doubt that which impinges most forcibly upon an individual.

Truth in art consists in those qualities which are not immediately discernible in things.

Fantasy takes on meanings in the light of underlying truth and belief.

"Hidayet has got brown eyes, black eyebrows and long brown hair. Her eye lashes are black. She has got pierced ears and a thin upper lip. She has an oval face and when she smiles she gets dimples. When she is angry she tells everybody to shut up. When she is sad her eyes water and she doesn't take any notice of what you are saying to her. When she is surprised her eyes twinkle."

RESPONDING TO A NEW EXPERIENCE

The reception class who produced the pictures of locust had been stimulated by a number of new experiences. Perhaps too many for one day.

A strange teacher, a new (to them) precision tool (a fine point fibre-pen), some dead locust and most exciting of all, each child had a new magnifying glass.

The latter caused much wonder. "They're all blurry." was heard, they needed induction into the mysteries of focus or elbow bending.

The task of recording what they saw proved absorbing. It also prompted a great deal of verbal enquiry. Many comments revealed surprising knowledge and unexpected insights into insects, geography and R.E.
The class were engaged in drawing and looking for a considerable time.

It was probably the first time they had been asked to make a response to an experience that was still being experienced and could be referred to and re-referred to.

Much of their previous work had been heavily dependent on their imperfect powers of recall. Very little use had been made of their growing reasoning skills and their ability to solve problems.

The few examples illustrated show, in a narrow age range, the wide variety of stages of development commonly encountered. As teachers we must be increasingly adept at learning from the traces learners leave of their learning.

Although this class had spent an unaccustomed time on this activity, they felt far from finished.

In their short school careers they had ingested the all too prevalent rule about "colouring it in". Sometimes it seems that work without colour is somehow inferior.

Colour provision in this particular situation was such that with the tools and materials available, the learning recorded in the drawings would be entirely obliterated with one or two marks.

At the next session, the children were directed to re-examine the insects and their colours, then, with pastel crayons, make a further response.

The initial try-outs with the marks the crayons made suggested a larger scale was appropriate.

The magnifiers and the insects were still available, also some new reference material but the children did not repeat their first drawings.

They had encountered the "need to extend the complexity of lauguage available to them", (Bullock).

They demonstrated their need to place the experience in a (for them) meaningful context. In their terms, "To make the locust feel at home."

The single example illustrated shows typical but not unconvincing evidence of the development of ideas and learning through Art.

The imagination initiates: it is the critical mind that creates.
Andre Gide, (1869–1951).

IMAGINATION AND FANTASY

When this image was shown to a group of young teachers on an induction course, it was put forward as an evocation of a very personal memory. A scorched and barren Greek island, full of heat, light and jagged rocks.

At the end of the session, a teacher told us she found the slide disturbing.

"I must be stupid," she said, "all I could see was a burnt, spiral notebook."

The advisory teacher was able to reassure her.

"You mind your fantasies and I'll mind mine," he said. "I will sometimes share mine, but do not seek to impose them on you. Don't therefore too strongly impose the fantasy of Lear, Potter or Dahl on your children. Share them, by all means but let the children develop their own, from their own responses to life." The next picture comes from an in-service "Learning Through Art" week course.

Simple basic materials and tools had been re-introduced and time allowed for familiarisation and "consumer research". This was related to a proposal that the teachers go out and respond to the environment.

A daunting task. To reduce the strain of so sudden an exposure to an unfamiliar learning situation, the teachers were told that they did not need to work outside.

They were encouraged to look for and if possible, return to base with some information or notes. Perhaps in the form of a fragment or an object that might represent, or stand for their response to The Elephant and Castle.

One teacher returned with an abandoned workman's boot. This teacher lacked confidence in her own abilities to use the materials which she had not directly experienced for many years. When the boot was placed on the table, on a piece of white paper, the teacher remarked that it looked silly and out of place. She was then sent down the fire-escape with a shovel, returning with a shovel full of "environment".

She was then in part, able to recreate the situation she was trying to respond to.

The boot meant very little without a context.

To her pleased surprise, she found in the course of her research that she had in fact, adequate skills. She was, with water colours and pastel crayons able to make a clear, would-be objective account of what she saw.

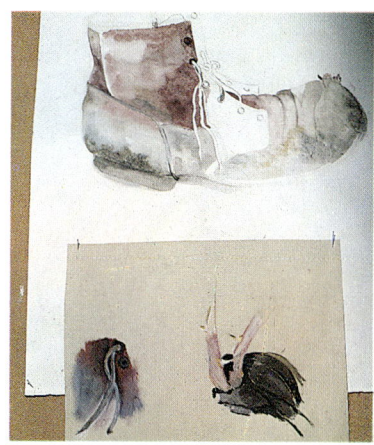

In a neglected corner of the advisory teachers' desk (for reasons unconnected with this project), was an old potato.
As neglected as the boot, it had begun to sprout.

The teacher noticed this.

Her personal, imaginative response to structural, colour and other affinities went beyond the initial objectivity. A very individual fantasy began to develop. It involved, amongst other things, sprouting boots and laced potatoes.

The structured ordering of these stages of development, alongside the growing control of media, provided language for individual expression

Fantasy, like all myth-making, is only one way of describing experience. It may in many cases be the only language to register the acute sense of a reality that has been lost, or a reality which is felt to lie beyond the deceptively straightforward surface of appearances.

Imagination is the ability to form an image not present to the senses, to invent, to discover.

"About my thorn pictures – I had been thinking about the crucifixion and my mind was preoccupied by the idea of thorns and the wounds made by thorns. In the country I began to notice thorn bushes and the structure of thorns, which pierced the air in all directions, their points establishing limits of aerial space. I made some drawings and in doing so a strange change took place. While preserving their normal life in space, the thorns rearranged themselves and became something else – a sort of paraphrase of the crucifixion and the Crucified Head."
Graham Sutherland, (1903–80).

"I will simply paint my bedroom. This time the colour shall do everything. By means of its simplicity it shall lend things a grand style, and shall suggest absolute peace and slumber to the spectator. In short the mere sight of the picture should be restful to the spirit, or better still, to the imagination. The walls are pale violet, the floor is covered with red tiles, the wood of the bed and of the chairs is a warm yellow. The sheets and the pillows are a light yellow-green, the quilt is scarlet, the window green. The washstand is orange, the wash-basin is blue, and the doors are mauve. That is all, there is nothing more in the room and the windows are closed. The very squareness of the furniture should intensify the impression of rest. As there is no white in the picture the frame should be white. This work will compensate me for the compulsory rest to which I have been condemned. I shall work at it all day long tomorrow." Vincent van Gogh, in a letter to his brother, 1888.

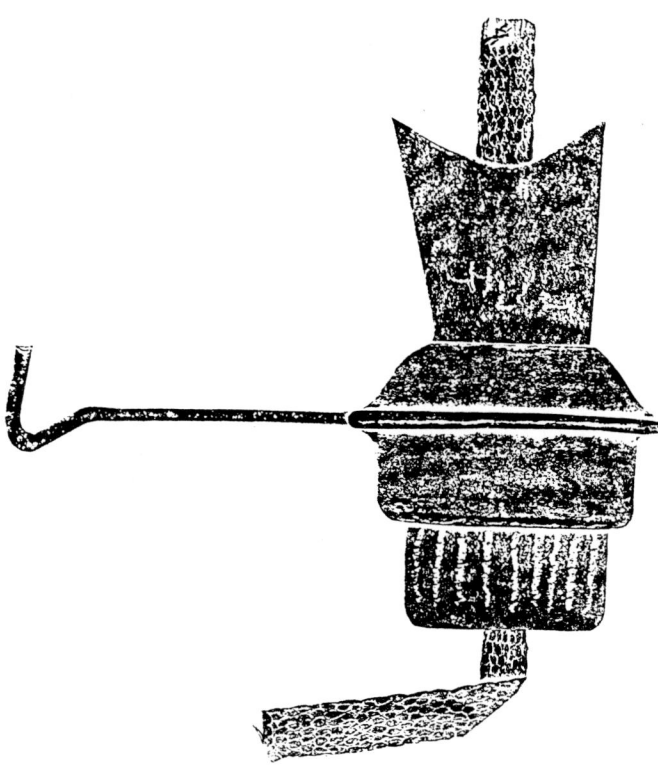

"The light of the body is the eye; if therefore thine eye be single, thy whole body shall be full of light."
Matthew 6.22.

EVALUATING ART IN THE PRIMARY SCHOOL

Art, through its range of functions in the Primary School Curriculum should be seen as contributing towards:

Reinforcement of concepts.

Development of ideas.

Appreciation of learning.

Sense of communal and personal purpose.

Acquisition of skills.

Ability to question, explain and discern.

Awareness of environmental, historical and cultural influences.

Confident ability to learn and retain knowledge.

To evaluate the contribution visual education may be making to the whole school policy it is necessary to look for evidence of:

A stimulating, engaging and relevant working environment with appropriate materials purposefully organised for learning.

Direct experience seen as a central starting point, allowing individual responses to be extended in relation to the learners' states of development and interests.

Progression as seen through a sequential examination of the processes, skills and needs the learner is encountering.

The above is applicable to the whole Primary School Curriculum. Art can be used as a central learning tool, particularly as so many learning experiences are initiated, developed, assimilated, questioned and reinforced visually.

No school or teacher can afford to regard so vital a resource as mere decoration.

"Quality is the continuing stimulus which our environment puts upon us to create the world in which we live. We invent responses to quality. Among these responses is an understanding of what we ourselves are. Art is high quality endeavour."
R. M. Pirsig, 1974.

"Leon Kossoff's approach involves constant striving, an ability to ride the turmoil and so win through to an acceptable degree of certainty. That's when he finally decides to reach for the fixative."
William Feaver.

"A result of contemporary exploration in education is the conclusion that educational experiment, in the main has been conducted and is being conducted in the dark - without feedback in usable form. The substitute for light (or usable feedback) is evaluation after the job has been completed. After the working party has been scattered, the evaluators enter. By then, it is so late in the day that only patching can be done. Indeed, such is the latitude in the choice of criteria for evaluation that something nice can usually be said about any course or curriculum. It would seem much more sensible to put evaluation into the picture before and during curriculum construction, as a form of intelligence operation to help the curriculum maker in his choice of material, in his approach, in his manner of setting tasks for the learner. Measurement follows understanding. If we have a sense of what is worth measuring, we shall measure better."
Jerome S. Bruner, Towards a Theory of Instruction, 1971.

"Are we to assume that all that children do is aesthetically valuable provided we have not guided them? By what criteria could such a judgement be made? Or is creative another word for enjoyable? If so, how is this to be justified as an alternative to learning? Is creative activity just a kind of free activity which is therapeutic for some children? If so, what about the rest? Or, finally, is the argument that free activity is good for promoting aesthetically satisfactory literature? But this must depend on the prior initiation of the person into the history and nature of literature, and an extensive experience of what has already been done. Where otherwise is the basis for any aesthetic judgement."
Keith Ebbutt, On Creativity, 1977.

EXTENDING LEARNING THROUGH ART

Extending educationally involves increasing the range and depth of learning experiences.

Extending learning requires increasing discernment, most closely related to the individuals linguistic development. Extending children must increase their ability to make appropriate use of information, experience and tools. None of this should be confused with novelty or embellishment. The processes embodied in the term "drawing" (whatever the materials or tools) can lead logically from initial stimulus and response, through recorded observations to further research and understanding.

From the beginning there is need for continual evaluation, modification and decision making.

A drawing is never a "first-draft", the second mark made, modifies and refines the learner's perceptions.

A valid learning project continuously produces alternative possibilities and choices.

Although it may be possible, even attractive to "sum up" the learner's findings, it is rarely appropriate to present a final solution in the form of a highly polished and disproportionately time consuming end-product.

At several stages it will be useful to present a thoughtfully ordered review of work in progress.

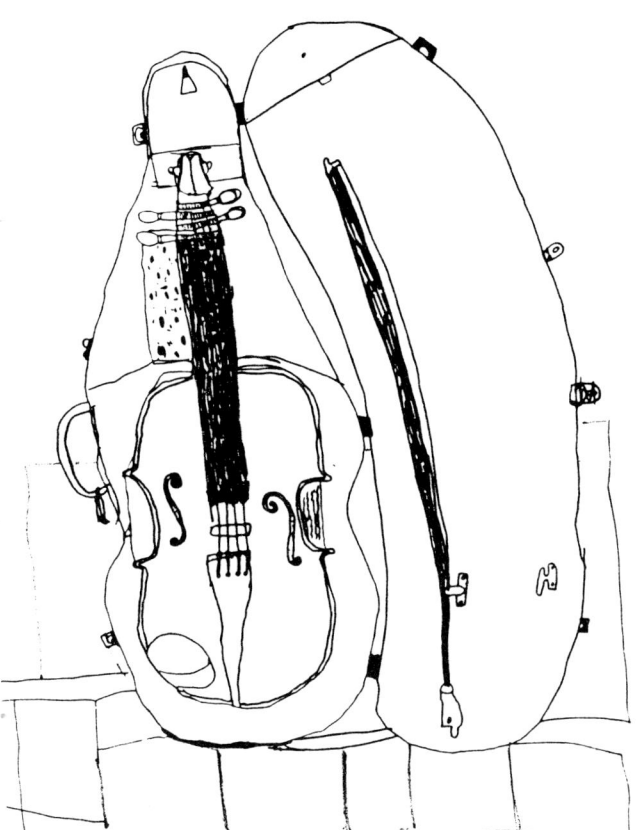

"Frames, out of all proportion to the matter enclosed in them – obviously an insufficient defence for the result of dissipation of effort and confusion of aim."
W. R. Sickert, 1915.

DISPLAY, SOME CONSIDERATIONS

As part of a stimulating learning ambience, the creation of displays of work, "finished" or in progress and displays of other aspects of our environment, enables learners and teachers to order their working area in a way that promotes the further development of their learning.

It also enables and encourages them to share their discoveries and to continue learning, aided by the responses of fellow learners.

Display can inform, enhance, excite, stimulate, reflect and question.

Display can acknowledge achievement, identify needs, reward effort, invite participation, demand engagement, command respect and assist evaluation.

All children may contribute to and participate in, decisions related to the appearance of their school.

Before we know where we are going, we need to know where we are. What better guide could we have than an ever changing and growing map that charts our learning as we learn? Drawings, as records of learning are almost always aesthetic objects. Aesthetic objects that do not record learning are probably ornament.

Careful and appropriate mounting of work helps us to see and neither distracts nor consumes time that might be spent in learning more.

Sheets of studies that show preliminary investigation can often be more informative as well as more useful than a highly finished presentation that may conceal the learning its creation has promoted.

SOME SIGNS OF PROGRESSION

These images all come from a primary school where the Headteacher and staff recognise the value of Art as a cross-curricular learning tool.

The pen drawings show children at different stages in the development of their understanding of line as a means of examining the shape and structure of objects like gym equipment and musical instruments.

The Indian images come from the preparation for a Diwali festival and use colour to respond to actual artefacts as well as other reference material.

The reception class paper print shows early skills being developed alongside the careful ordering of simple shapes from a previously constructed Lego model. Later we see the confidence to tackle the more complex forms of a violin. Throughout this book we have generally avoided giving chronological ages. We hope that teachers might develop their ability to watch for developmental progression so that children continually encounter the need to extend themselves.

"Art for Art's Sake is a piece of slang that does not mean the harmless thing it seems to mean.

An art cultivated professedly by a few, and for a few, who would consider it necessary – a duty, if they could admit duties – to despise the common herd, to guard carefully every approach to their palace of art."
William Morris Address to the Trades Guild of Learning, 1887.

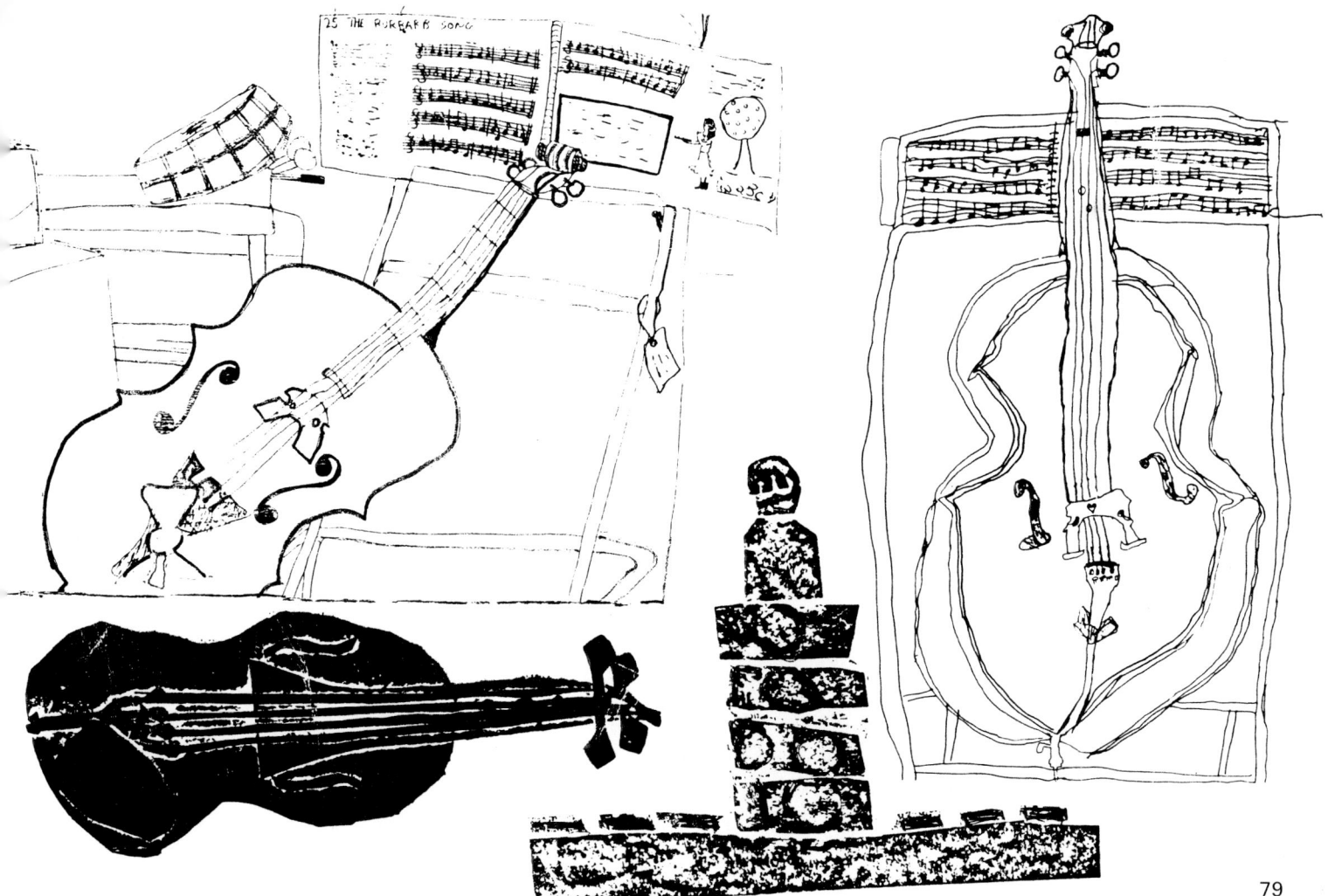

LOOKING FORWARD – EXTENDING DRAWING

This book has emphasised the wide ranging functions of Art in a primary curriculum, using as starting points the central disciplines and skills loosely described as drawing and painting. Any other activity aimed at and intended to meet the learner's needs, to extend the range and complexity of expressive forms available may be equally valid.

However, other activities, using other materials and techniques must surely justify their place in a balanced curriculum. They must also genuinely satisfy the evaluative criteria herein proposed as foundation study.

Is a print or a model more valuable for learning than a drawing simply because other materials and techniques are used? The novelty value of new materials can easily be over emphasised. The most truly transferable skills are surely thinking and reasoning skills.

In the following step-by-step description of a simple form of print making, the values implicit in this way of seeing are examined as an extension of drawing.

Print making as a way of learning to look

When learners experience and question an aspect of their environment or an individual object, a great deal of preconditioning by other images may inhibit their ability to respond directly to its meaning. A simple form of print making may be a possible alternative to more traditional forms of representation. It may also, at another stage, extend the range of these forms while increasing the learner's confidence.

To begin, we require: Two pieces of thick A4 paper (grey and white brushwork), scissors, a quick drying and easily applied glue (pva used sparingly with a spreader), a thick black wax crayon, a supply of thin bank, duplicating paper or newsprint cut to A4.

Later we will require a formica or perspex off-cut (40 × 20 cm), an inking roller (15 × 5 cm), a tube of black water based printing ink and a spoon for burnishing.

The initial aim will be to investigate, through looking at the shape and structure of an object, or part of an object, natural or man-made.

When the extended simple skills of this particular method have been acquired, it will be found that these skills can be applied to more complex and individual problems encountered by learners in everyday experience.

The object is examined and its important features are selected and identified. It will have been chosen initially for qualities of shape and structure rather than colour and for its potential capacity to motivate and stimulate enquiry and active engagement. It will probably make connections with other learning areas. This engagement will be prolonged and reinforced as component shapes are isolated and an attempt is tentatively made to record them by simply tearing or cutting them from one of the pieces of thick brushwork paper.

Questions of size and scale will certainly arise. What are we looking at? What do we know? What can we find out? Which aspects are important? Do we need more information? What is this part called? What is it like? What interests me?

The shapes selected and cut can be arranged on the other sheet of thick brushwork paper and ordered, modified and added to. With the black wax crayon, a rubbing carefully taken on a sheet of thin bank paper might clarify and solidify the shapes. It will soon become appropriate to glue the shapes into position to avoid confusion.

Gradually, step by step, the image is developed.

There is no suggestion of failure while the options for further investigation and modification remain.

The periodic test rubbing will show a steady progression towards resolution and might even be numbered in sequence.

There will be a need to gain finer control over the rubbing process. Marks scored with a ball-pen might be added.

The image may be found to be less dependant upon unconfident linear guesses than the learner's previous experience with other drawing materials.

The initial stimulus continues to provide information.

At a suitable stage, a crisper, clearer representation of the image than the wax rubbing offers may be called for.

Now, an ink print can be taken.

The black water based printing ink is evenly rolled onto a square area of the formica or perspex off-cut (resting on newspaper). The evenly inked roller is then used to evenly distribute a thin coating of ink onto the cut and glued image ("the block"). To avoid congestion, there should be an inking area adjoining a printing area where the inked block is now placed, ink side up on a sheet of newspaper.

Now a print can be taken on a piece of thin A4 bank or newsprint. The back of the firmly held down print is evenly burnished. A spare roller may be used to augment the spoon. As long as the block and the print are firmly held, a tentative peep-preview may be allowed.

A second inking will probably give a clearer result as the re-inked block becomes primed.

At each stage the result so far achieved can be examined and evaluated in relation to the initial aims and intentions and modification, clarification and refinement can be continuously attempted. The temporarily acceptable solution is often more useful than a final solution.

A SUMMING UP

If the approaches and proposals of **A Tool For Learning** are to be implemented and developed, teachers will need to discuss with their colleagues what changes are needed and to assess their current practice.

Taking direct experience learning as their starting point, they will need to formulate a whole school policy and agree upon a common philosophy of curriculum development.

This will be essential if the children are to feel secure as they progress through the school.

It is also the vital factor if any progression is to be percieved.

This policy, strongly rooted in practical classroom organisation and environmental awareness, need not aim at standardisation or uniformity. Rather an agreed common objective. Let the learners learn.

People have recorded experience for a long time. Art history is the story of civilisation. We can learn much from looking at records of other people's learning. Source materials in school should be the most authentic we can find. .

Books and postcards reproducing drawings can often be more valuable than those confined to presenting a finished product which may appear to have occurred "ready made", without trace of doubt or struggle. Such images do not often inspire confidence in the learner.

These drawings from one of Vincent van Gogh's sketchbooks show an early stage in the planning that led to a series of paintings.

TOOLS FOR LEARNING

In recent years, large areas of the Primary School Curriculum has been taught through the project method.

There have even been lists produced of the "Top Ten" projects (Costume Through the Ages, Transport Through the Ages and Dinosaurs).

Too often the emphasis has been too heavily placed on the content.

Projects should not be seen as merely fact-amassing.

Children need to learn research skills.

Many children simply copy verbatim from the over simplified information books they are given.

A recent enquiry* examined a large sample of the popular information books.

The researcher concluded that the resulting activity could best be described as "Making notes from notes."

When selecting books for children to learn from, great care must be taken to ensure that they are not only appropriate for the developmental stage, but that they fulfil the basic requirements of any reference.

To be usable at any level, a reference book must present its information in an ordered and accessible way.

Too many books lack one or more of the basic essentials such as: Index, contents list, publisher's "blurb" or summary, bibliography or further reading list, introduction, glossary, text-

* "Making notes from notes", I.L.E.A. Contact, 21.11.86.

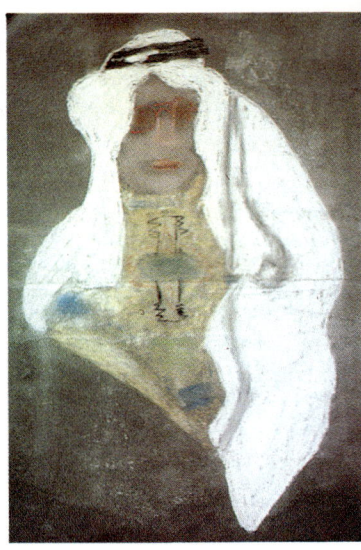

related captions to pictures and clear headings and sub-headings.

Many of the books aimed at the project market do not trust children's ability to understand the richly diverse range of imagery that is often to be encountered in what might be described as prime sources.

Books that make use of authentic, contemporary illustrations are often neglected in favour of stylised, colourful and decorative images that are mistakenly believed to appeal to all children.

It is a chastening but useful exercise for us as teachers to try to learn from the inadequate tools that we have sometimes been persuaded, are good enough for children.

A NOTE ON ILLUSTRATION

To be both creative and educational, projects which use Art and Design as a main element must stimulate, motivate and engage the learner.

If the teacher is to do more than merely direct the child to produce a regurgitated, imperfectly recalled stereotype, time must be allowed to research, prepare and provide appropriate resources.

When the function is mainly to illustrate and to express the learner's own response to story telling, the visual aspects of the cultural and historical context may be directly experienced through contact with available, authentic artefacts as well as existing (i.e. previously imagined) illustration.

To reproduce without meaning is meaningless.

Two pieces of writing from a desert project.

"We worked from the real thing. We got a bucket of sand and some cacti. Each table had some sand, African and American cacti, toy camels and some little model white houses. We arranged our sand, cacti, houses and camels in the way we liked. We used chalk pastels on black brushwork paper. The pastels were dry like the sand. We tried mixing colours on test sheets. I tested out the colour of the sand and then the cacti. The camel was the hardest bit and it was quite difficult to know where to start. I started at the top of the highest cactus so that I wouldn't put my sleeve in the pastels."

"There are two types of deserts, a cold desert and a hot desert ... The Sahara is a hot desert and the north and south poles are cold deserts ... The camel is sometimes called the ship of the desert because it carries food, people and clothes across the desert ... Some of the desert dwellers live in tents made of goat hair, others in simple houses that are painted white. White reflects heat and light so keeps the interior cool ..."

Mary Newland and Maurice Rubens wish to thank many teachers and learners for drawings, prints, advice and inspiration, they include; Athelney Primary School, Bellingham, Alexander McLeod Primary School, Plumstead, Annandale Primary School, Maze Hill, Bessemer Grange Junior School, East Dulwich, The Cathedral School of St. Saviours and St. Mary Overie, Southwark, Cubitt Town Infants School, Isle of Dogs, The Charles Darwin Memorial, Downe, Kent, Eltham Church of England Primary School, Eltham, Gordonbrock Infants School, Brockley, Hungerford Infants School, Islington, I.L.E.A. Saturday Classes and 'Learning Through Art' In-Service Courses, Kidbrooke Park Junior School, Kidbrooke, The Lakeside Health Centre, Thamesmead, Montbelle Primary School, New Eltham, Pickhurst Infants School, Bromley, St. Anselm's Primary School, Tooting Bec, St. Clement Danes Primary School, Covent Garden, St. Luke's Primary School, Norwood, St. Peter's Primary School, Hammersmith, Shaftesbury Park Primary School, Lavender Hill, Southlake Primary School, Thamesmead and POS Ernst Thalmann, Bautzen G.D.R.

"actual size" detail *drawing* p 7 8

SOME USEFUL BOOKS

Children's Drawings, Jacqueline Goodnow, Fontana, 1983
Ways of Seeing, John Berger, Penguin, 1972
The Story of Art, E. H. Gombrich, Phaidon, 1986
(Or any single illustrated volume that surveys two or three thousand years of learning through looking.)
The Story of Modern Art, Norbert Lynton, Phaidon, 1980
Community and Creativity, John F. Friend, Bretton Hall, 1975
David Hockney on Modern Art, An interview with M. Bragg, ILEA Learning Materials, 1981
Images for Life, Natural History Museum, 1970
Drawing, Philip Rawson, OUP, 1969
Arts in Schools, Calouste Gulbenkian Foundation, 1980
Art and Science, Dolf Rieser, Studio Vista, 1972
Drawing, Technique and Purpose, Susan Lambert, Trefoil/V&A, 1984

Mrs Brown running and laughing

wax rubbing

ink print

AFTERWORD

Good learners have confidence in their ability to learn.

If they fail they are not incapacitated.

Good learners rely on their own judgement; They are not afraid of being wrong.

They can change their minds.

Good learners are not always fast answerers: they may delay judgement until they have more information.

Good learners are flexible, they will change their viewpoints and have another look.

Good learners understand that answers are relative: What is true now may not be true later.

They respect facts but know that facts are tentative.

They can make distinctions between statements based on facts and other kinds of statements.

Good learners are skilled in enquiry.

They question assumptions and use definitions and metaphors as instruments for thinking.

Good learners continually try to verify their beliefs.

They are good observers and understand that language can obscure differences as well as control perceptions.

Good learners do not demand an absolute final solution.

"I don't know doesn't depress them, it stimulates them."

Drawings are often more informative and less distorted by reproduction than other works of art. They may also reveal more of the learning processes embodied in their making.

Some books show "actual size" details of paintings. These too, can sometimes show more of the artists' methods and intentions.

The images in this book have been chosen to amplify the statements. They were all produced in a range of learning situations and with a variety of intentions and functions.

None of the images were made especially for this book and some may convey different meanings in their present context. Selection was in some cases directed by printing considerations and some have been reduced in size.

Different intentions, skills and stages of development are sometimes apparent without reference to age.

In a recent lecture, we showed two slides.

One was a typical piece of "child art". It had a caption supplied by the teacher. This stated "Andrew (5 years) saw a crane knocking down a building". The next slide had no caption.

We suggested one. It was "Paul (63 years) looked from his window and saw a mountain". We do not suggest that Paul is infantile, nor do we suggest that Andrew is an artist.

We do, however, insist that they are both engaged, at very different stages of development on a very similar, if not identical activity.

They are encountering and experiencing their world and trying to make sense of it.

NOTES

NOTES

NOTES

NOTES

NOTES